You Can

Make It

Young Women:

How I Survived

Mildred Henderson

"You Can Make It Young Women: How I Survived"

ISBN 978-1-7360684-5-8

Author: Mildred Henderson
Editor: April Johnson
AJ Creative Writing Coach & Editor -
www.ajcreativewrites.com

TABLE of CONTENT

Introduction

I was born in 1927 to a sharecropper in Minden, Louisiana. My mother died when I was fifteen months old. I grew up with loving grandparents, who became my guardian after my mom died. I married at an early age to an abusive man. I thought it was a part of love and marriage. Even though my grandparents never fought in my presence. I don't know why I equated love with abuse. Parents respected their children and didn't fight in front of them, as they do today. I had the privilege to live during segregation and after integration. I have four children that I adore and never deserted. I was taught resilience at an early age. I know from experience that you can make it if you try. Times may get hard, but hard times will pass if you have faith in God. My family's values are founded on Christian principles. My grandparents trained me to follow these principles. Some of the taught principles were, yes ma'am, no ma'am, thank you, and always be obedient to the family rules and respect all adults.

I survived a divorce. All four of my children graduated high school. Two of my children continued to community college. I did not have enough money to send all my children to college, but they understood. I kept my family together with love. It took a lot of love and prayers to endure hard times. It was worth every sacrifice I put in to invest in my children.

I am ninety-three years old. I retired from the Internal Revenue Service (IRS) years ago. I was a foster parent for eleven years. I am presently a health care provider. I take care of patients that can't take care of themselves. I became a foster parent to help children who endured harsh abuse due to their biological mothers giving up on life. They felt they couldn't face life's adversities. If you have a little faith the size of a mustard seed, you can make it. God will see you through.

I emphasize "young women" because I look at many young women who give up on life at an early age. I fostered all ages and races, and their problems were the same, neglect. The children became a part of our lives. I hope and pray we had a lasting impression on the children. I wanted the children to know that someone cared for them. I pray that some of the children will remember what we aimed to teach them.

Prologue

I started watching the Oprah show. I saw so many young women having such a hard time coping with life until I thought I should write a book. If someone sees what an experience I had in life, it might inspire them to go on. If I tell my story, it might encourage them to go on with their lives. I know if I could make it this far with all I have gone through, I know they can make it. Things are much different now. Even when we rode the Greyhound bus to town, we had to stand up when all the back seats were taken. There were two rows of seats in the back for us colored folks. Even if there were empty seats in the other bus sections, we had to stand up when they filled up. If their sections filled up, and a white person needed a seat, someone in our area had to get up and give up their seat.

White men formed groups to beat or kill black men, and no one did anything about it. There was just another dark person gone. If I lived through that kind of life, I know young women can make it in today's society.

So many people didn't know what the good life, so to speak was. You can't miss what you never had. Some people had property left to them by their parents. They wanted to stay to make a change for their families.

Whatever places we went in, everything was separate; little dirty dark restroom for us to use in some old building. Drinking fountain; there was a sign, white on one and black on the other one. You better not get them mixed up. Movie theatre, the blacks were upstairs in the dark. The whites were downstairs. Then they cut us out altogether. I worked for white women, and I had to enter through the back door. I could go all over her house to clean it.

When we walked downtown on the sidewalk, we had to step off the sidewalk so they could pass when nearing or approaching a white person. If it rained, we had to step in the water or the mud; just as long as we didn't touch the white person. We couldn't try on clothes; we weren't clean enough. We have come a long way, but we still have a long way to go. I lived through some rough times, but God brought me through. I was taught at home to carry myself. I taught my children the same principles, even though they lived out West. Segregation changed things, but the underline suddenness is still in some places. We are slipping back to some old ways, but our young people don't see it because they haven't been there before. I hope and pray we won't let history repeat itself.

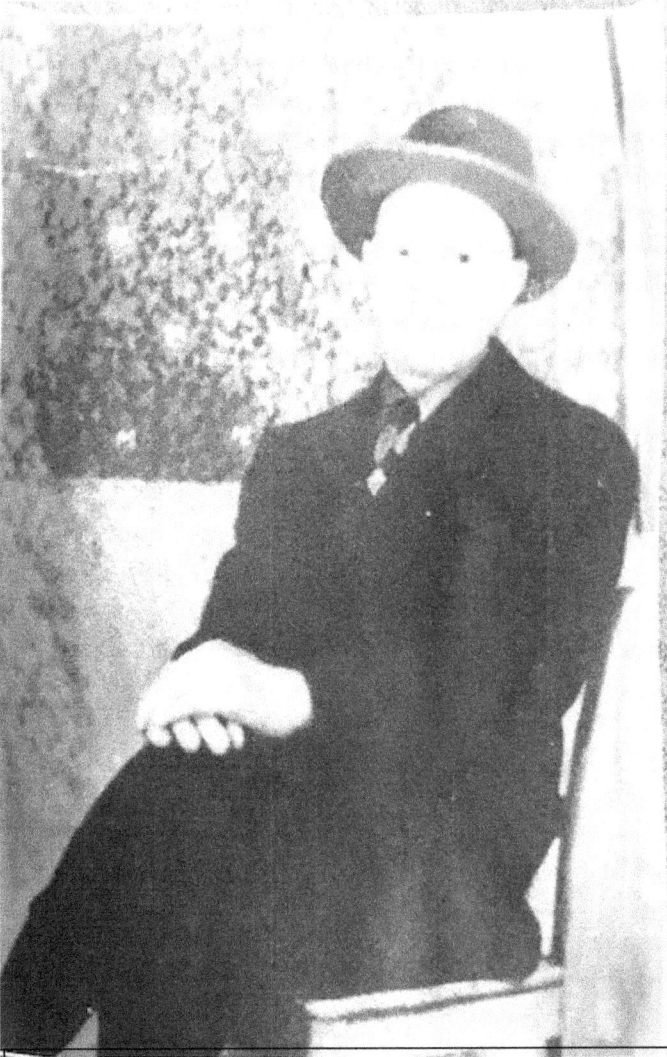

My Dad

Chapter 1

I was born in a little town called Minden, Louisiana, on June 3, 1927. My parents were sharecroppers. I am the youngest of three children. After my dad married my mother, he moved from the farm to town. His dad had a family farm where my dad grew up. They farmed a variety of crops. My dad was Albino with freckles. Albino is a genetic condition that causes an absence of pigment because of the defective gene(s) affecting the melanin in the skin, hair, and eyes. When my grandmother was pregnant, she said she saw a man who was an Albino. My grandmother laughed at him, and when my dad was born, he looked just like that man. People believed in karma at that time. If you made fun of something or someone, your child would reap the seed you had sown. When daddy moved to town, he found work at a local train station. It was a little easier for him to find employment because of his skin color. Dad bought a house for the family in Minden. My mother did housework for white families. After about eight years of working, my mother became ill. Shortly after becoming ill, my mother died. No one ever discussed her illness. When she died, my brother was nine years old. He remembered our mother. He told me the doctor performed surgery on my mother on our dining table, and she never recovered. My sister was six years old. And I was fifteen months.

Dad had a lot of life changes after the death of my mother. He lost the house, took my brother, sister, and moved in with my granddad's sister. My dad's parents took me in to live with them. My grandmother told me a dream she had before my mother's death. My grandmother said, "She saw my mother running toward a stream of muddy water, and just before she got to the wattle, mother was carrying me in her arms." She said mother stopped long enough to hand me to my grandmother, and she ran into the muddy water and drowned. Granny said she made a promise to mother in the dream that she would take care of me. My grandparents were amazing to me. My dad's sister had eight children. She was a single mother due to a failed marriage. My grandparents purchased our family home in the early 1930s. We all grew up together in the same household. I was the baby of the whole family. The youngest cousin was nine years older than me. The family protected and spoiled me.

I never lived around the boss, so to speak, or the white folks. My grandfather owned the land we lived and farmed on. I did not know we were poor. So, we did not go around them for too much. My grandfather was the son of a sharecropper. His mother was a full blood Indian. I do not know what tribe. Granddad was a man of short stature, with brown skin complexion, and straight black hair. I often combed and scratched his scalp, which he loved. After granddad married my grandmother, his dad arranged for him to buy one hundred-twenty acreage of land. I do not know if the two houses were there when the property was purchased. The two houses on the property were not the same size. One was larger than the other. My grandparents lived in the largest house because our family was more substantial. My grandparents, my aunt, her eight children, and I lived in the house together. My dad and his other sister live in the smaller home. My dad's two sisters married two brothers, and both marriages ended in divorce. My dad moved away from the family home when he remarried. My dad came back home after his second marriage failed. The one hundred twenty acres of land was plenty of space to farm crops. Granddad farmed and raised cattle and chickens to supply the family with meat. He grew vegetables, fruit, and melons. He also raised cattle, chickens, and horses. There were sugar canes as well. We did not want for food. The only food we needed to buy was rice, spices, salt, sugar, and flour. The family made cornmeal from the corn that was grown in the field. The corn was taken to the grinding mill to grind into cornmeal, then bagged, put into a can, or brought back home to cook.

There were wild plums, sometimes clusters of trees, we called plum orchards. In the summer, you could pick plums by the buckets. We did not have to buy fruit during the summer. We had apples, peaches, pears, fig-trees, wild grapes, dewberries, and blackberry vines. In late summer or early fall, we had fruit on vines that looked like large grapes, but they were muscadine. Muscadine is a type of grapevine that is grown in the south-central and southeastern United States. We ate as many as we wanted, then granny made jelly out of the rest. Granny gave away jars of jelly to families that did not have fruit trees on their land.

In the early 1930s, granddad bought a new Ford Model T car, although he never learned to drive. One of my older cousins drove granddad's new car. I do not remember which one. I was too young, but I remember we all piled up and packed ourselves in that little car to ride to church. My granddad did not ride with us to church. He walked. He enjoyed walking to places in the community. We were a happy family. We lived about one-half mile from the church. We rode around on the farm in the wagon before we went to church in the car, or sometimes, we walked to church with granddad.

My first years in elementary school was fun. My cousin taught me my ABCs and how to count to one hundred before I started school. I was six years old when I started school. My cousins were still in school, but they attended another school for older children. I attended a three-room schoolhouse. One classroom was for beginners, preprimary to second grade, which is now kindergarten. The next classroom was the third and fourth-grade room, which was taught by my cousin.

In the mornings, my cousins walked me partially to school. I could see the school when they turned around. When school ended, they met me before I entered the woods. I had to walk across a long log through a creek. I was afraid to walk home alone. I thought I was going to fall into the water. I walked past a deep blue hole, where granny fished. The trail was so close to the edge of the deep part of the water. The path went up the hill to the edge of the bank. When it was cold, granny dressed me nice and warm. I had to wear long underwear, long sleeves, and pants. I hated them. I waited until my cousin turned around, and I pulled the underwear up out of my stockings and rolled them up to my hips. When school was over, I pulled them back down where granny had put them. I did know she was trying to protect me from the cold.

The African-American schools always received used outdated books from white folks' schools. To receive new books was unlikely. The books were handed down to us. Despite the secondhand books, we always learned our school lesson. At night, I laid on the floor and read by the kerosene lamplight. We used kerosene lamps as our lights. We did not have any knowledge of electric power. I always had plenty of help with my homework. They taught me how to write, as well. I always enjoyed school. Some of my friends and younger cousins walked the same path going to school. We had fun walking to school and home from school. I sometimes had to run and catch up with the other children. One day a group of my classmates was walking home from school. We were close to one of the girl's houses that were walking with us. A man suddenly appeared and called her name just before we approached the woods near her home. We all ran. I told my cousin what happened. I did not think any more about it. A few days after the incident happened, my folks came a little closer to the school to meet me. After a few days passed, a white man was at the house when I got home from school. He was talking to granddad, and they were waiting for me to come home. Granddad told me the man wanted to talk to me. I said, "Yes, sir!" He asked, "What happened after school when the man appeared near the woods?"

I told him I did not know. The only thing I could say to him was, the man called my friend's name near the woods, and all of us ran. After that day, all of us children had to go into town and tell them what we saw. I was so afraid. My folks drove me into town. I had to go into a small room where ten to twelve white men sat in chairs. They questioned me about what I saw. When we left, I asked my folks what is this about? They did not tell me. I found out at school a few days later that the man had raped my classmate. She did not come back to school. The man was her stepfather.

When I was growing up, you did not hear about rapes and crime too often. I felt safe wherever I went, but I also know that someone was always with me to protect me. There was always someone at home with me. There was not much stealing because no one came around stealing what you owned when we left home. I guess the reason is people freely gave to one another and was always willing to help.

Chapter 2

In 1936, granddad had a stroke. He went to see a boss man that lived across the way from us. I did not know at the time, but I found out later that granddad owed the man some money that he could not repay at the time. Granddad was on his way back home, and the man said he was going to take his horses, mules, and cows for the money. We were right in the middle of plowing at the time. He was trying to get to home but kept falling.

He made it close enough for me to see him. I called my male cousins to let them know something was wrong with granddad. My cousins went to meet him and brought him home. He was sick and could not walk well. Granny put him to bed and used home remedies to help him get well. We could not afford to go to the doctor every time someone was sick. We found out later granddad had a stroke. The next day a man came over to the house accompanied by others. They drove off with every horse, mule, and cow we owned. Granddad had raised the farm animals from babies. To finish reaping the crops, my cousins had to go over to the man's house and rent our stock to complete the summer harvest. They rented our cows for milk. The crop was finished and given to the man, but he said it was not enough to pay the debt. Then he took the land my granddad owned.

The rest of the time we lived there, we had to pay rent to the man, and he owned everything in the house. Losing everything was too much for granddad to handle. He started to lose hope. That was my first life change. He lived about another year and a half and worried the whole time until he died an early death. He had another stroke while visiting my dad.

Before all this happened, my granddad and I used to have lots of fun. My chores were feeding the chickens, gathering the eggs, helping grandma pick food in the garden for the family dinner. The older children worked in the field from Monday morning until Friday afternoon. After lunch on Fridays, the girls helped grandma wash, clean the house, and scrub the floors. We did not do too much on Saturday. They cleaned the yard and went into town on Saturday evening. The clothes were washed outside in a large aluminum tub, also known as a tin tub. We boiled water outside in a large black pot. First, we ignited the fire. Then we put the pot on the fire to warm the water. Once the water was warm, we poured the water into the tub over the dirty clothes to rub on a scrub board. We did not know what washing machines were. After we scrubbed the clothes, we put the clothes in a pot to boil the excessive dirt. We made sure the clothes were nice and clean. After we took the clothes out of the pot, we put the clothes back into the cold-water tub with a long cleaning stick to avoid burning ourselves. A few liquid blue drops were placed in the water to ensure the white clothes were sparkling white. The blue liquid came in a small bottle from the store.

You put a few drops in the water. It turned the water blue. Your clothes looked as if you used Clorox.

Most families at that time made their soap for laundry detergent. Making laundry detergent took place in the yard outside the house. We used the fat from meat that was fried and mixed it with a white grain substance. The name of it was Eagle Lye. I do not know what else they put in the mixture. They boiled the formula in a black pot until it was thick. The mixture was left to cool. After it cooled, we stored the liquid soap in a large tin can. When wash day came, the clothes were put into a tub of warm water. We applied the homemade soap to the stubborn stain and rubbed it on the scrub board. After rinsing the clothes two or three times, the clothes were hung on a long line to dry outside in the sun. After the clothes dried in the sun, they were taken down off the clothesline and brought inside the house to be ironed and put away.

A rubboard is a board that had a piece of tin with nailed ridges on the board. The board had two legs slanted back diagonally and stood on its own in the tub. You would take one piece of clothing at a time and rub up and down until the dirty stain was gone. It was hard work, but the process cleaned clothes thoroughly. The clothes were cleaner than using a washing machine.

My first experience with a washing machine did not go too well. I had never seen a washing machine before. I was sent to this nice woman's house to wash her clothes. They didn't have to wash their clothes by hand like us. The washing machine was a white round tub with a dasher in the center and with four legs. I thought this was so neat. There was a wringer that stood over the top of the machine, that you moved around. It also had a removable lid cover to prevent the water from splashing on the floor. The lady showed me how to use the machine. I put warm water in the washing machine with the soap they purchased. Then I put the clothes inside the washing machine. I pulled the handle on the washing machine's side, and the dasher started to twist backward and forward. Once I thought the clothes were clean, I pushed the handle in the opposite direction to stop the wringer from dashing. Lastly, I open the lid and put the clothes in the wringer.

I smoothed the clothes out as she showed me. I kept my hand on the garment and turned on the wringer. I forgot to remove my hand, so I smashed my hand in the wringer. I cried out loud. The lady came to my rescue by reaching inside the washing machine and unlocking the wringer to release my hand. My hand was hurt and in excruciating pain, but I had to finish the laundry. I rinsed the clothes by putting the clothes inside another tub. Once I rinsed the clothes, I put the clothes back through the wringer to wring out the excess water. Then the clothes were ready to be taken outside and hung on the clothesline.

The only soap we purchased at our house was for bathing. The homemade soap was much too strong. It would have blistered our skin. We only took baths on Saturday evenings in the washtub. We heated the water in a black pot outside, brought the heated water inside, put it into the washtub, and bathed. We used the multi-purpose tub for washing clothes and bathing. The tub was round and not large enough for an adult to sit down in, but that was the only thing we had to use.

We used a washbasin to wash our private parts and feet from Sunday to Friday. We did not wear shoes during the summer months because the dirt seeped in our shoes while working in the field outside. After working in the dirty field, we had to take a pan bath and go to bed.

Chapter 3

There was a stand built against the wall. It was to hold the water bucket. In this bucket, everyone drank from the dipper. As soon as we entered the house from the backdoor, it was mandatory to wash our hands in the washbasin when we entered the house. We had to wash our hands before going into the kitchen and before every meal. Most of the time, the dipper was homemade. We made the dipper from a cut, bent tin can. The tin can was strategically bent around a circular pattern, not to cut anyone's mouth. We turned the seam of the tin can in a downward curved position to make the handle. This prevented your hand from getting cut. When a homemade dipper was not made, granny purchased a new dipper. Another way to make a homemade dipper was from something that looked like yellow squash. After removing the inside of the squash looking substance, we hung the homemade dipper out to dry. Once the dipper dried, we used it to drink. No one ever became ill from drinking from the same dipper.

Grandma kept a towel hanging on a nail against the wall in the kitchen by the backdoor to dry your hands. Our water source was from a well that was dug in the yard. A box was built around the well so nothing would fall into the water. There was also a top built over the well. When you pulled the lid back, there was a counter for the water bucket to sit on. A rope was connected to a wheel to click the well to draw water from the well. We pulled the water from the well so the animals could drink water at night. Water was needed for the house and the chickens as well. The water was crisp, clean, and cold. Granny would seek out a particular grass to make homemade brooms to sweep the floor. The grass was sturdy, stiff, and swept the floors clean. When granny didn't make her homemade brooms, we purchased a new broom from the store. Saturday's, we swept the yards too. The yards were pretty white sand, like the beach. We had lots of large trees in the yard, especially in the front. The evenings were cool from shade from the trees. Granny also cooked her meal for Sunday dinner on Saturday's. The family rule was no cooking on Sundays. The food never spoiled. Sunday dinners always included the preacher, or the preacher and his family from a different community. We also had family members that didn't live close to the church for dinner. We had many insects, so I had to standby the table and fan the insects away while the adults ate. When out of town relatives visit, we shared our meals. We also shared our meals with almost everyone in the community. We considered them as our cousins as well.

Granny always cooked an abundance of food. We still had plenty of food to serve everyone. Granny enjoyed preparing the food and cooking for Sunday guests, especially the preacher. There were fun times. Sometimes they sat at the table and talked for long periods after they finished their meal. Although I was hungry, I had to wait until the adults finished their meal and left the room before eating dinner. We addressed most of the community's older adults as uncles and aunts—my cousins' dated people outside our community. When a new young man visited my cousin, the first thing the older folks said was howdy, who's your folks? What are their names? They wanted to make sure the grandchildren were not dating a relative.

My cousins were old enough to have boyfriends. When a girl became fifteen, they could take a company that is what they called it. The boys came to the house to see the girls. No one could sit close to one another or close the door to the room. The old folks were going to hear and see what was going on in the next room. I wanted to see what was going on, too; I always tried to get their attention. My grandmother was a firm disciplinarian. If she made a promise, she tried to keep the promise. She was an example to the children to do likewise. She had a memory like an elephant and would often remind you of the promise she made. You could depend on that. If she promised me a whipping, she was not going to change her mind. I hope she would forget about the whipping she promised, but she kept her promise and whipped me when she felt like it. I preferred to get my whipping immediately. If I lied to her, she punished me as soon as she found out the truth.

When I was in fourth grade, I was in a play at school. I wanted and needed some new shoes. We had plenty of food, but very little money to buy clothes and shoes for nine children. My school shoes were a bit run down and out of season. Being in the school play was an unforgettable night for me. When I got a pair of new shoes for spring, they had to last all summer for Sunday church.

The night of the play, the shoes hurt my feet so badly, I cried. I could not tell granny. The summer was coming, and I was going to be barefoot all summer. My feet were getting bigger, and I had to wear those shoes to church every Sunday all summer. I wore the shoes to church and took them off as soon as I sat down. As soon as Sunday service was over, I took the shoes off and walked around barefoot.

I now know she was teaching me not to be a liar. If I told her the truth, I am sure she would have gotten me another pair of shoes. My thoughts were if it took two weeks for the catalog order to arrive, it would take the same time to return the shoes. That would have taken more than three days. That's the mind of a child; they think they know it all. I learned a lesson I will never forget. I have corns on my toes today because of that learning experience. Two pairs of shoes a year was about the most we could expect and afford, but I was happy. Every family around us was in the same financial situation. I didn't feel ashamed.

Mildred in 1955

Chapter 4

We lived in a rural area of Louisiana. The houses were far apart due to the broad acres of land and pastures of grass and woods. The yard was spacious with a white picket fence and a white sandy yard. This convinced our parents that we didn't need shoes in the summer. Summertime was a fun-time for us. We got plenty of sunshine and fresh air from playing in the yard most days. We completed all chores before going outside to play.

We did not own a television. We used the radio for entertainment. We had a big old fashion radio that picked up some local stations. There was no such thing as couch potatoes. We played fun games like Hiding-Go-Seek, Hopscotch, Ring-Around-The-Rosy, and other yard games. I loved working in the flower garden with granny. She always had beautiful vegetables and flowers.

We manicured the lawn Friday evenings or Saturday mornings. Cutting the grass and keeping maintenance of the yard was hard labor. We did not have a lawnmower. We used a hoe to cut the grass. After we cut the grass, we raked the grass into a pile, picked up the stack, and transported the pile to be burned. We did this once a week. I was taught discipline by doing my chores. I learned to balance. It was a time to work and a time to play. My folks said an idle mind was the devil's workshop; therefore, we were kept busy with chores.

Before my granddad became unable to work, he was a very active man. He and the older men in the community went to the woods and cut down trees to make tables, chairs, and wooden beds. We didn't have to buy a lot of furniture. We used the smaller tree limbs for chair backs and legs. The men trimmed and carved the wood with pocketknives until the wood was smooth. They sat on the porch until late at night, carving and talking.

My Granddad slaughtered cows and took the cowskin to make cowhide for the seat of the chairs. The chairs were well-built and lasted for years. No one ever fell through the bottom of the chair. Even a large person didn't have to worry about breaking the chair. The slaughtered cows' hide was stretched and left in the sun to dry. The cowhide had various uses.

The meat was cooked and canned for the winter from the same cow. Canning the meat was a method used when it was too cold to kill the winter's wild game. The canned meat made good pot roast. Hot biscuits, rice, and peas that all came from the barn, and supper was ready. My granny didn't like too much wild meat. Sometimes she cooked a rabbit that the fellows brought home. I didn't eat wild game until I was grown and married.

When I think about it, we didn't need a lot of money. Our farm and granddad hunting skills provided the livelihood for us to survive. When the weather was inclement, the men worked inside. They worked and talked about old times. This was a time of working and storytelling. The children enjoyed cutting and eating watermelon. After we ate watermelon, granny saved the rinds to make watermelon preserves. The rinds were washed and cut, put into a large container, and covered with sugar to sit overnight to draw out the juice. The next day it was placed on the stove and cooked until the liquid thickened like syrup. The preserves were put into jars and stored in the storehouse on the shelf for the winter. Ready to be open later to eat. On a cold winter morning, granny prepared breakfast. She cooked homemade hot buttered biscuits, sausages, and sometimes eggs. I considered this good eating. Granny also made preserves out of peaches and pears. To this day, I still make different preserves. According to the New England Journal of Medicine, we are not supposed to have too many sweets in today's world. Articles show the harmful effect sugar has on our health. The sugarcane that grew was taken to the syrup mill and processed into syrup. We produced two kinds of sugarcanes: saccharum and ribbon. The ribbon cane always has the best taste. The saccharum cane was not as sweet. Granddad took the boys to the bottom. The bottom was the lower part of the ground near the pasture, where it stayed damp. They stripped and cut the cane down to the grown. The cane was loaded onto the wagon and taken to the syrup mill. The syrup mill had a machine that squeezed juice out of the cane. They put the sugarcane through the machine, hooked up the mule to turn the device. The machine had a long tong(tongue). One end hooked to the machine. The other end was attached to the mule. The mule walked around and around in a circle. Then you fed the cane into the machine. There was a large container sitting under the machine to catch the juice. The mule walked until all the canes were grounded up. There was a large fireplace or similar made of bricks, with a large hole in the middle. We lit a fire under the bottom, and flames came through the top. There was a large square pan that held ten or twelve gallons of juice. The cane juice was put in this pan and cooked until it was thick. This was real syrup. The syrup was put into containers and stored for winter. Granny wanted the ribbon canes in cans and the saccharum cane in jugs. We brought the syrup home and stored it in the smokehouse. It was my job to keep the kitchen stocked. We sometimes served syrup, biscuits, eggs, and rice for breakfast. Sometimes cookies were baked and put in a bucket. They hung the bucket on a nail on the wall in the kitchen. We had permission to take a few snacks. We always had to ask an adult for permission to take anything from the kitchen. We stored teacakes the same way. My granny loved sweet foods, so did I, and still do. The sugarcanes we didn't use were cut down and laid straight in a long trench, covered with dirt. We used this process so the sugarcane would grow for the next year.

The men kept themselves busy, so did the women. The women would sew a lot in the winter. The women took scraps of small material to make clothes. They also took scraps from old clothes and cut them in different sizes and patterns to make quilt tops to cover the bed. They made star patterns and many other patterns. These quilts were large enough to cover beds like the comforters we buy today. But with better material.

They were made by the older women that stayed home and took care of the younger children. The quilts were made with love, put together with patience, and lasted a long time. Grandpa brought home sacks of flour for food and to feed the cattle. The sacks were washed and bleached and used for the bottom of the quilts or clothing. Grandpa got cotton from the cotton gin to put between the top and bottom. A lovely warm quilt was made for the cold weather.

Grandpa bought large fifty-pound sacks. This made a large piece of strong material. The quilts were useful, beautiful, and large enough for the bed. You could cover your head and tuck it under the foot of the bed. They were also wide enough to hang over each side of the bed. The women exchanged patterns with one another. Sometimes they gave away scraps, mainly to large family's scraps. People were good about giving to help one another. We shared food, clothes, or anything we had with others. They bought large sacks of fertilizer, the sacks were open at each end, and down one side. This made one large piece of material. It took about four sacks to make one cover. The women also made clothes for needy families. The community looked out for widows, broken homes, and families with children. There was no welfare at that time. My grandmother loved to bring gifts to people when she heard someone was ill and needed help. Grandma gave the children whatever that was needed from the storehouse. We gathered the neighbors' food requested from the storehouse. We played outside until we had to go into the house. I loved to play. We were not allowed to sit around and listen to grown folks' conversations. That was a no-no. After supper, we sat, peeled, and canned fruit and stored them in fruit jars in summer. At our house, we all sat and ate together. We cleaned the kitchen after a meal and put everything away for the next day. Granny canned fruits were better than the fruit we buy from the stores. It was clean and full of love. This is more than I can say for what we buy from the store today. We made our pillows at home. We made them from the loose cotton that grandpa brought home from the cotton gin. Sometimes we made the pillows from chicken feathers. The mattress we slept on was also homemade. They purchased blue stripe material from the store and sewed each side and both ends. The center split was left open at the top fill with cotton. After I got a little older, we went into town to a large warehouse. Granny and the older adults made the mattresses. They looked more like the mattresses we purchase from the store. The ways we eat breakfast today were not the way we ate breakfast when I was growing up. Today everyone looks out for themselves, and everyone is subject to eat something different. Granny woke up early to make sure everyone ate a good hot meal. The boys woke up and started a fire in the woodstove. They made homemade biscuits every morning, eggs, bacon, or sausages, or both, and rice. We always had plenty of milk, butter, jelly, and syrup. We stopped what we were doing, came to the table, sat together, and ate our meal. We always said grace before each meal. Things have changed in some families. On freezing cold winter days, grandpa, relatives, and friends from the community would kill six to eight hogs. The day had to be cold, so the hog meat would not spoil—this provided meat for the family to eat and share with the community. We always gave away plenty of milk and butter because we had so much of it. Sometimes we produced five or six gallons of milk a day because we had plenty of cows. We milked the cows twice a day, mornings and evenings.

My grandpa always fastened the hogs up in the pen and fed them corn, water, and milk we had to throw out. The hogs were cleaned, fatten, and prepared for the table. Hog killing days were big at our house. It took a team of men and women to prepare for the process speedily. Grandpa built a high stand ahead of time. It was needed to hang the hogs up after being killed and put in hot water to remove the skin hairs when scrubbed. A large barrel had to be washed and cleaned. A stand was built for the barrel to lay in a slant position. Tubs were lined up and ready to use. The women heated the black washpot on the fire until the water boiled. Large pans were prepared, and a fire was made in the kitchen's stove, the work began. The men killed the hogs one by one. There was a large moll on the other side of a single blade ax; this was used to hit the hogs in the head. He was left on the ground to die. When they were sure the hog was dead, he was removed from the ground and put into hot water in the barrel, headfirst. They pulled the hog out of the water, flipped him around, and put him back in hot water. When this process was over, the hog was taken out of the barrel. A stick was cut and put through the back of the hog legs so he could be hung on the high stand, high enough to put a tub on the ground to catch all his guts. The hog was scraped clean, and all his hair was removed. Then the hog was washed down before preparing to cut him. When the hog was completely clean, a large butcher knife was used to cut the hog. They started cutting from the bottom of the stomach, through the chin. The women separated everything; I mean everything. The live heard, and the lutes were put on a bench. They were washed and put into a pot with onion, garlic, salt, and pepper to make hash. The hog's stomach called the hog maws, and the intestine was cleaned out and washed in another tub. Now the hog is ready to be cut up. The feet were cut off, put into a pan, scraped by the women. They cleaned all the hair off the hog before cooking. The hog huff was cut off and saved to make tea when someone became ill with a cold. Sometimes the feet were cooked and canned. It depended on how many hogs were killed that day. Sometimes half of the feet were given away. The head was cut off and cleaned—hog head cheese was made. We called south meat from the head. The bead and the tail were cut up, seasoned with all kinds of spices and vinegar to make the hog head cheese.

I never saw the cows slaughtering process. They were taken somewhere else and killed. This man had a large canner, where they cooked the meat and canned it at the same place. When they brought the meat home, it was canned and ready to be stored in the storehouse. When they wanted canned beef for dinner, it was ready to be warmed up. They didn't pack beef away like they did pork.

We had a small house that was called the smokehouse. We packed the fresh meat in salt. This was salt they used, especially for curing meat. The meat was packed in large wooden boxes and covered for an extended period. I don't know how long the process took place. The women packed down the ham, shoulder, and bacon. The old folk called that the middling and pork jowl.

When the men packed down the meat long enough, it was taken out of the box and hung on a wire hook in the smokehouse. Hickory wood was placed in a container, and a fire was started, and the flame was smothered. The purpose of the process was for the smoke to fill the smokehouse. After the procedure, they allowed a few days or weeks to pass for the meat to get cured and ready to eat. We cut a piece of ham and eat it without cooking it on the stove. The men killed the animals at the start of the winter. The meat lasted until the middle or last day of summer. There was no refrigeration or icebox.

The sausage's meat was cut into small pieces and ground in a grinder and hung on the wall. We used the same machine to stuff the ground mixture into the small intestinal that the women washed. Then we hung the sausage in the smokehouse to be smoked. We had smoked and linked sausages. The intestinal were soaked in vinegar water to take away the odor. Then, they were ready to be stuffed with sausage meat. They washed and rinsed it several times. The women boiled the large intestines in salt, pepper, and garlic, and fried. We now called them chitterlings. My dad said he used to be in the restaurant, and they were called Kansas City Wrinkles. All lean scraps were grounded for sausage. Some of the links were fired into a pan sausage and put into jars. We had a meat supply all year round, and we didn't have to buy from the store.

Granny picked fresh green peas from the field to cook. Some of the peas were canned. The remaining was dried and put into the barn. The peas were put into the barn to dry completely. If they were left out in the rain, they mildewed. When the peas were dry, they were taken out and put in the wagon. On a bright, cold, windy day, we spread the peas out in the bottom of the wagon, and we beat them with a long stick. The stick was somewhat like a baseball bat. The peas were whip to break-up the shell from the dry peas.

When the shells were broken from the peas, a tib was put on the ground. The bucket was filled with peas and broken shells. We stood on the wagon and held the bucket up high and pout all out of the bucket. The shells flew away, and the peas fell into the tub; neat thing, don't you think? I told you my grandpa was smart. Some vegetables grew summer and winter, like collard, mustard, and turnip greens. All the other vegetables were canned for a later day. We had a canner that was used to can all the food. In the fall of the year, we gathered nuts for the winter. We grew pecan trees in the yard, black walnut trees, and hickory nuts. There were chestnut trees grown in the pasture, but we called the nut chinquapin. The nut was a little smaller than the chestnut. They had such a good taste to them.

At Christmas time, granny bought what we called English walnut, Brazil nut, which we called nigger heels, and almonds. This took place once a year. She bought raisins with seeds inside. You could buy them in boxes. They were sweet and crunchy.

I didn't have to crack my food; grandpa snapped them for me. They thought I would smash my fingers with the hammer. When he could no longer crack them, he would tell my cousins to crack them for me. They would do it for me because if they didn't, I would tell grandpa, and he would make them do it. They had me spoiled. After all, I was the baby.

Chapter 5

Christmas was always a fun time for me. Granny made me go to bed early. She told me Santa Claus was coming. He wouldn't come to the house if I didn't go to bed. I believed that for a long time, and then I found out differently. My cousin went to the pasture to get a green holly tree with red berries on it. We didn't know anything about Christmas lights. Above the mantle was a green vine that was over the fireplace. The smell of food saturated the house. Granny always made sure oranges and fruit were in the fruit bowls. They told me Santa Claus was coming down the chimney, but they never lit the fireplace.

I woke up early on Christmas morning. Grandpa had the fire burning in the fireplace. Grandma and my aunt were cooking in the kitchen. I ran into the living room to see what gifts were left for me. Most of the time, it was a doll and some clothes for winter. I was happy and grateful for the gifts. As a child, I believed my grandma and aunt cut the cakes and pies for Santa. The old folks stayed up late and ate cake themselves. We visited our relatives' houses to see what they cooked, and most of the time, we ate their food. Granny cooked five or six different cakes and several pies. She baked a whole ham and cooked chicken, stuffing, and trimmings. Granny took food to the elderly family members who could not cook for themselves. My cousins roasted the peanuts in the fireplace. They cooked the potatoes and peanut in hot ashes and stirred them until the peanuts and potatoes were cooked. We also cooked them in the oven. We ate them while they were hot and drank milk. Sometimes, somebody would pass gas, and you would have to leave the room so the room could air out, but it was fun.

When it snowed, we made ice cream from the snow. In the summer, granny made her homemade ice cream. Granny would have the boys to bring ice from town. We had an ice cream freezer with a crank attached. Once you turned the crank, it didn't take long to make the ice cream. You had to put plenty of ice cream salt over the ice.

We never had to purchase butter. We made butter from cows' milk. We churned the milk to process butter. The milk was put in a stone jar to set for two days. The milk clabbered. You could drink it or wait until the milk churned. We had a wooden handle that resembled a broom handle with two nailed wood pieces, like a Christmas tree stand. The wooden handle was washed and put into the milk. The stone jar held five gallons of milk. It had a top with a hole in the middle to fit over the stand and cover the milk so that it wouldn't splash. The dasher was pulled up and pushed back down into the milk until butter formed on top. That's how we made fresh butter when needed.

We skimmed the butter off the top of the milk. Then we put the butter into a bowl. We rinsed the butter with cold water to remove all the milk. After rinsing all the milk off the butter, we added salt to the butter to keep it from tasting fresh. We put the butter into the water bucket. Then we placed the water bucket into the well to stay fresh. We used the well for our refrigerator. If we made too much butter, we feed the hogs and offered milk to the neighbors that did not own cows.

We did not know about water heaters. The sun was our heater. We poured water into a tub and sat it in the sun all day. We used the water for whatever reason needed. In winter, we heated water on the stove. Our bedrooms were freezing cold. The fireplace only warmed the nearest rooms. Granny or my cousin warmed an old piece of blanket or a quilt and laid it in the bed for me to lay on it. The warming method made the bed warm and cozy.

We did not have a bathroom in the house. We used night pots with lids for our waste at night. We called the pots slop jars. We used the lids to control the odor. We emptied them in the outhouse the next morning. The outhouse was a little house with a seat built in it to use the bathroom. There was a deep hole in the ground to catch the waste.

I was the person selected to bring the pots in every evening. I intentionally past the door to the company room, where my cousins and their boyfriends were. I put two pots in each hand to bang together an attract attention. Although I wanted to see what they were doing, I couldn't go into the room. My cousins would get so ashamed and angry at me. Granny was not going to let them whip me. That was fun for me. I could have gone into another door, but that would have been no fun.

Chapter 6

Grandpa was older and couldn't go to the field anymore after the stroke, so he became my playmate. He was the love of my life. Granny would sometime go out and work in the field for a while after she made lunch, which was called dinner during that time. I made sure grandpa was well-taken care. We babysat one another. He walked on crutches. The stroke didn't affect his mind. He had a very sharp mind. Sometimes granny went out of town to a church meeting and stayed a few days. Auntie was always home to cook. I was glad to see granny come home because she sometimes brought me something back.

When everyone left the house and went back to the field, it was grandpa and me. I thought of things to do to make him laugh. I sometimes went to the barn to get corn to feed the chickens in the yard. The weather was nice and warm. We sat on the porch or under the big oak tree. When chickens eat and get full, they start to release themselves. I took corn and stuck it in their feces. I like to see the chickens try to eat it out of the mess. The chickens tried to shake off the waste. This was funny to grandpa. We both had a good laugh out of watching the chickens. I was told that chickens eat anything. This was not funny to my cousins because they had to clean up the yard.

My grandpa was a mild-mannered man. He loved his grandchildren dearly. He spent time playing and talking to us. Grandma was sterner. She was the disciplinarian of the family. Grandpa was getting weak. He worried about not paying the debt he borrowed from the man who had taken everything from us. I heard him and granny talking sometimes. He always needed money for supplies in spring for the next crop. He was getting deeper in debt. Grandpa was affected deeply by this debt. He was never the same. My dad and aunt convinced grandpa to visit them at their house. Grandpa stayed two weeks at a time. My dad remarried, and my brother and sister lived with him and his wife. My aunt moved to another community.

When grandpa went away, I felt too lonely until he came home again.

When I think about it, it was good he spent time away from home. I was prepared for his final trip. He never came back home. It wasn't too much longer. He had another stroke and died at dad's home. My sister had a dream two weeks before his death, and his death happened just like she dreamed it would. She told my mom the dream, and mom told her it was just a dream, don't worry about it. I lost the dad I loved so much. He gave me the love and values that I have today. He taught me so much. Most of all, he taught me to love.

Funerals were different in the 1930s. They embalmed the body at the funeral home. The wake was at the home of the deceased the night before the funeral. People sat up with the family throughout the night. That was a sad day at our house for me. I couldn't stay out of the room where he was lying. I was afraid of the dead, but grandpa was different. I knew he wouldn't hurt me. After my grandpa left me, my whole life changed. It was grandma and me. I know she worried and missed him as I did. She was not my playmate like grandpa. She didn't play with us children as he did. She stayed busy around the house. I had to play by myself.

Granny started to visit people that were in need or ill more often. I am sure this helped her take her mind off of her problems. She did a lot of church work. She lived about a year in a half after grandpa's death before she died. Oh, how my life changed. I had to move from the only home I had ever known. All my cousins married and moved away from the big house, except one. He was married, but he stayed in the house until the old folks were gone.

My stepmother and granny had a good relationship. Mother told granny some of the things that dad was doing to her. Granny disapproved of daddy mistreating his wife. Granny told my mother not to take that mess off dad. I was always close around. I heard what was going on. My dad liked to chase other women. I knew that about him. I often overheard granny and my aunt talking about him. They didn't think I was listening. My dad fathered two daughters outside his marriage with my birth mother. The oldest girl often bragged about the things' dad did for her. When she came to church, she showed other children what he bought her. Dad didn't talk about his children by the other woman until their stepdad died. Someone would have gotten hurt. Sunday, the oldest girl came to church wearing a pretty black dress. The dress had some pretty designs across the front. She told someone that she knew my mom would find out about the new dress. The next week mom told my grandma. The same day he purchased the dress for my older sister. He bought five yards of material that cost him fifty cents. It was ten cents a yard. It looked like a lining.

Granny asked to see the material. Mom brought it to her. When granny saw the material, she said I wouldn't wear that. They didn't think I was in the next room. Dad never told mom when he did something for the girls. He never did anything special for mom. Granny didn't like to see anyone mistreated, not even by her son.

Growing up, we did not have a telephone. But that didn't stop news from traveling fast. We could go to church on Sunday, and someone would tell granny about an illness in the community. The next week, the news had spread around town like a wildfire. When we heard the news, we went to the garden, pick greens, killed and fry a chicken. Make homemade bread, and sometimes bake a cake. A box or basket of food would be prepared to take to the family that was ill. She knew the family could always use a good hot meal, mainly if it were a mother that was ill.

Granny went to the sick person's house and helped out wherever needed. She made sure there was food for the whole family. There was so much love and concern in the community when I grew up. Everyone did not have access or could afford to go to the doctor. There were many home remedies that we used. People prayed over one another, and they would get well.

I still use some of the remedies today. There were herbs in some of the plants in the pasture that was available for use. There was a plant that was called Mullein. The herbal tea from the plant mullein help cures horrible coughs. We boiled the plant with cow's waste. The tea name is called cow chip tea. We saved the jawbone from a hog for the grease on the bone to rub over the jaw when we had the mumps. There were lots more that I wish could remember.

I moved with my dad right before I turned twelve years old after my grandparents died. I only lived with my dad when I was a baby, right before my birth mom died. He was nothing like my grandpa. He didn't provide for his family as grandpa. He only looked out for himself. I resented him for a long time for the way he treated me. My dad's focus was on planning cotton for us to work. He didn't think about winter was coming, and we needed food to be stored away. There was no one to handle the massive fields of cotton except mom and me. I had to work the fields from sunup to sundown. There was no more

Friday afternoon's off. It was only three of us picking cotton. Mom and I didn't get a dime. I loved my mom very much. She was always good to me.

Mother taught me how to share. When I lived at home with my grandparents, there were no other children to share with others. So, everything was mine. Then I went to live with my dad and mom. One day mom took some of my writing papers, and I became upset. She set me down and told me I needed to learn how to share with others. She explained everything that was given to me was not just for me alone. It was also for me to share with others. She always shared with me. That taught me a lesson that I have never forgotten.

It was canning time; mom was looking for fruit to can. We always got fruit from Uncle Alex. Mom and I walked over to Uncle Alex's house. He lived down the field. When mom was tired, she sat on the porch and sent me to the field where Uncle Alex worked. She told me to ask him if he had any peaches for the year. I went to the field and talked to Uncle Alex about everything except peaches. When we finished talking, I sat under the tree and never looked up at the fruit. I left Uncle Alex in the field and walked up the hill toward the house. All of a sudden, I remembered why I went to talk to Uncle Alex. I stopped, thought to myself, and said, he doesn't have any peaches. When I got back to where mom was waiting, she asked me if Uncle Alex had any peaches. I said no, not this year. It was dreadfully hot, and I didn't want to turn around.

Uncle Alex came over to the house a few days later. I was in the kitchen, churning milk to make butter. Mother said to Uncle Alex. I am sorry you don't have any peaches this year. I depended on your fruit trees. Now neither of us has any fruit. Uncle Alex said, what, my trees did better than they ever had before. My heart started to pound. I knew I got caught in a lie.

Uncle Alex asks who told you I didn't have any peaches. Mom called me in the room, didn't you tell me, and Uncle Alex said he didn't have any peaches? I said, "Yes, ma'am." Uncle Alex said, "That gal didn't ask me anything about any peaches."

Mom said, "She was under the trees." I knew I had a whipping coming. I deserved just what I received. I never forgot to ask about the fruit again.

Mother and I worked hard in the field all week because we wanted to get up early on Saturday and get our work done before going to town. Daddy hooked up the mules to the wagon and put a seat across the front for him and mom to sit on. I placed an old piece of a quilt on the wagon's floor to sit on, and off to town we went. Sometimes mom and I had to work in someone else's field when our work at home was complete. We had time to eat a cookie and drink a soda.

My mother loved to drink a large RC Cola. I was ashamed to consume the large soda. I would get a small Coke Cola. I asked the store clerk; may I please have a Coke? We hooked up the mules and wagons outside the back of the store. The colored folks were allowed to sit behind the store and cool off and talk to one another.

You could buy a drink for $0.10, and a stage plank (a large cookie) was $0.03. We were full when we finished eating. We met up with my other cousins and classmates. We walked up and down the street to window shop. We wished we had money to buy what we saw. This was our pleasure time. Many teens and adults met near Main Street, by the back alley, next door to colored folk's restroom. The folks danced and made out in this area. I was not allowed to go in there, but I slipped in anyway. The children were not allowed to go into the dance hall. We went to the restroom and then snuck in the back door. Thank goodness there was a back door. I met my boyfriend there and watched the front door. Every so often, my dad came. The lights were dim, so when I saw my dad come in the front, I went out the back door and ran around the corner with mom.

Chapter 7

Before Christmas, my cousin and one of her classmates picked me up and rode into town to the Five and Dime Store. I saw a little car I wanted, but I didn't have any money. I asked my cousin if she could buy it for me. My cousin's friend said she would buy the car. We approached the checkout counter. My cousin purchased her items. I waited for her friend to pay for the car, but she didn't. I grabbed her by her coattail and rode her coattail out the door. I tried to get her to buy the car, but she said, "Come on out of here." The lady didn't know what was going on. When we got outside the store, she told me we would not bring you to town anymore. You will get me taken to jail.

I didn't want to go with my cousin's friend anymore. I didn't know she was going to steal the car. I went home and told my aunt what happened. I was taught to ask for what you want, and don't take anything that didn't belong to you. Sometimes we traveled to town on Saturdays. We stayed later than expected. We did not make it off the road before dark. We had no streetlights during this era. I was afraid the cars were going to run into us. I sat in the back of the wagon on the floor and held the lantern lights so the cars could see us. We called this the taillight holder. Sometimes the cars would get so close to us before they would go around us.

We bought sugar, salt, spices, rice, and whatever else mom had the money for on our trips to town. When we arrived home, dad took care of the mules. I fastened the chickens, and mom put away the food. We opened the unlocked door. During that era, we didn't lock doors. No one ever went into your house and stole your belongings. Saturday evenings, we prepared for Sunday. There was no work done on that day.

Food was cooked and left out overnight without spoiling. Some people had iceboxes, but we did not. An iceman delivered ice two or three times a week. The milkman delivered milk three times a week. We lived in the rural part of town. We didn't have that luxury. The people who lived in town paid for everything they purchased. They worked for white families, and that's how they got their money. We didn't have to pay for things like that, because we had a farm.

I now hear about child labor laws. I often wonder where that law was when people my age were growing up. Children worked in the fields all day long. No one became ill from the sun. Now they tell me you can die from heatstroke. I have lived in the city for many years now, and I find myself complaining about the heat. I have bought into city life.

God protected us from the heat. He knew we didn't have a choice. Some children didn't have to work as we did. We were still in bondage and had to work from dawn until sundown. I pulled six feet long, seventy- five-to-one-hundred-pound cotton sacks. I carried buckets of water in each hand at the same time. I lived before central air and heat was invented. I am 89 years old, and in good health, so my doctor says.

I have worked hard in the cold, carrying wood for the stove and fireplace to keep warm and avoid freezing. We had to get up and go to the barn to get whatever food was needed.

Sometimes it was cold. We would have to blow on our fingers to warm them up. But oh, God brought me through.

I had to work in the field before going to school. I milked the cows and turn them out into the pasture. I brought the milk inside and gave it to mom. She took care of it. I had to feed the chickens and turn them out of the chicken house for the day. The hogs had to be fed and turned out as well. Then I had to get ready for school. Mom had breakfast prepared by the time I finished my work. I ate breakfast before going to school. We prepared slop in a large barrel for the hog pen. We gathered food scraps from the tables, and leftovers, mixed with milk.

It was hard work to dip from the barrel and carry it to the hog pen and pour it in a trough. If I didn't go to school, I worked in the field. When I got home from school in the evening, I repeated the same duties. I also got a basket, gathered the eggs, and took them inside. If there were baby chicks hatched while I was in the field, I had to provide a place for them.

My dad was hard to get along with, and he didn't seem like he loved anyone except my sister. After my mother's death, his second marriage did not last very long. I never spent any time with that wife. I met her one time. Dad was still living in town when they got married, and we were living in the country. I heard the old folks say she didn't like my brother and sister.

When I came to live with my dad, he was married to his third wife. She had no children. She was always nice to me from the beginning. My brother and sister remembered our mom, and they weren't welcoming to my dad's wife. I supposed they had memories from the second wife. Mom said she had a bad first marriage. She left her first husband and moved from Louisiana to Texas to get away from him. Mom told granny about her first marriage. When he got ready to leave the house, he took the broom and swept away the tracks after he backed his car out of the yard. Mom's first husband left the broom outside the gate and looked for tracks when he returned home. If he saw any tracks, he whipped her like a child.

The night dad married his third wife. I was still living at grannies. We all went up to my aunt's house and waited for them. We stayed up until he brought her home. That's where dad was living at the time. When she walked in the door, I said hi, mother. Mom said afterward she was frightened and surprised at my greeting. My brother didn't call her anything for a long time. He would walk in the room and start talking. She broke him from acting like that by not responding. Then he started calling her mother.

Dad soon moved out into a place of his own. When I came to live with him, both my brother and sister were gone. There were never any problems with my mom and me. I was looking for another mom because granny was gone. My sister never accepted mom. She fought with her all of the time. She got pregnant and left home at fifteen. After the baby was born, she was in and out of the house.

Mother and I worked hard to finish chopping our cotton. We chopped cotton for people in the community. We were paid twenty-five cents a day from the white folks and fifty cents a day from others. When we finished picking cotton and gathering food at the end of the year, we had time to grow a lot of vegetables. We had no money for school clothes. Dad never brought his money home to provide for the family. He spent his money on himself. He had to ask for money to get started at the beginning of each year. The money he earned was from feeding the rented mules and fertilizer the crops. Sometimes dad turned in fifteen or twenty bales of cotton. The boss said you almost made it out of debt, but not entirely. He started over again and never made any progress.

We worked hard all summer, chopping, picking cotton. Then come winter, we cut wood in the cold weather and snow, to keep the house warm and cook with the wood. The Boys chopped wood and brought it to grandpa's house. There were no electric lights for us at nighttime. There were times when mom and I had to go to the woods and help dad cut the wood. Then dad brought the wood home. We had to cut it up in smaller pieces before we could get it inside the house. The boys also took care of the horses, mule, and cows. Mom, dad, and I had to share the work at dad's house. I grew up fast. Mom also took care of the washing. She made sheets and clothes out of sacks, and the printed sheets were made from dresses. Mom gathered some of her old dresses from when she and dad first married. She gave the dresses to a seamstress to alter for me. I needed dresses for church and school. We weren't allowed to wear pants. Mom also worked in the white folk's house, so they gave her clothes I could fit. She sometimes made enough money to buy me a pair of shoes. The shoes cost $1.98. The clothes that were given to mom from her job looked better than the sack clothes. The lady was going to throw the clothes away.

I lived with dad and mom for four years until I couldn't take it anymore. Dad turned their four-room house into a boarding house. I'm not sure how much each person paid dad. Dad and mom slept in one room that was called the company room. They had a bed, dresser, and couch in their room. The sofa was named a state. The bedroom I slept in had two beds. Dad and mom slept in the room with me when we had company. We ate our meals in the third room. The third room had a bed, a table, four chairs, and a cabinet where we kept the dishes. This was called the dining room. Dad rented out the dining room since it had a bed in there. We had one cousin that had separated from his wife; he stayed there a while. Whatever they paid mom, and I didn't get any parts of the money. We had to clean up behind the renters. The renters didn't help us in the field or around the house.

One of my mom's nephews lived with us for a while. He was a big help to dad. He helped whenever and wherever needed. He talked dad into buying a car. Dad couldn't see well enough to drive. He was nearsighted, most Albino's are. Mom's nephew drove dad around town. That was good for a while. We didn't have to go to town and church in a wagon. The young man wanted to see his girlfriend, but dad wanted to be in the car all the time.

Dad and the young man started not to get along too well. He said dad took him to the field and talked terrible to him. He told his sisters about dad's verbal abuse. So, they came and got him and sent him to Seattle, Washington. He went to live with his oldest sister. After he left, I had no one to talk to that was my age. I was not old enough to drive. Dad wouldn't have let me drive anyway. Dad sold the car because no one lived with us could drive.

I was allowed to go live with one of my cousins and go to school from her house. She lived near the high school I attended. I grew up with my cousin. My first year in high school, what a year I had. This was great, no one to fuss at me. I could walk to school with my friends. I could stay with my cousin from Monday through Friday. Then I went back home on the weekends.

My cousin was married with two children. I loved my cousin so much. She was always fun to be around. She knew what I had to go through at home. She allowed me to have more freedom than I had at home. I stayed after school to attend the ball games, homework with my friend, and I hung out after school. She trusted me to do the right thing. I didn't let her down. Neither did I let me down. I knew the consequences. She let me wear some of her clothes on special occasions. I didn't want to go back home when the school year ended. My parents moved further out in the country where we previously lived. We could walk to town. We had to walk about three miles to the mailbox that was on the main highway. The mailman delivered mail once or twice a week. No one lived close to me to associate with, neither male nor female. We had an old radio that played sometimes. We had an old record player we had to wind up.

Chapter 8

**1955, Mildred in the Center
with Two Friends**

I was fourteen years old when I met my first boyfriend in 1941 while living with my cousin. His name was Reuben. He was on the basketball team. Our basketball team always beat the opposing school teams in the area. I enjoyed this year as a teenager. Reuben walked me home after the games were over.

My brother and sister were alumni of the high school I attended. They left their wild marks there. I had to be very careful because dad would have made me come home if he heard I acted out of character. I did not want to leave before the end of the school year. I would have had to walk too far to get to the other high school.

My boyfriend and I broke up before the end of the school year because we had a misunderstanding. We never really got back together. That was a bad experience for me. Reuben was my first real love. When we had a ball game at school, I stayed after school with my friend. She lived close to where I stayed. After the game was over, we all walked home together. Reuben and I went to my house, sit on the porch, talked, and made out.

The freedom to have fun without being afraid I was doing something wrong was liberating. We had a misunderstanding on commencement Sunday for the senior class. Reuben was a junior. After the program was over, the juniors cleaned up behind the seniors. Reuben went inside to help clean up, but he stayed a long time. I knew I had to get home because I wanted to come back to the dance. I sent a young man inside to tell Reuben I was ready to go home. The young man came back and told me he could not find him. So, I did not wait any longer. I left school and started to walk down the road. Another young man who tried to pursue me began walking with me. We were walking and talking. Reuben came outside of the school building, looking for me. The young man I sent into the school to tell Reuben I was ready to go, he told Reuben I had left with someone else. Reuben caught up with us. He wanted to know why I didn't wait for him. I told him what Bob had told me. He said Bob didn't come and tell him anything. I didn't believe him, and he didn't believe me. That was the beginning of our breakup. It was near the end of the school year. It was also near the end of my first love relationship. I didn't want the confusion and tension in our relationship. I went home, laid down, and cried. I wanted to tell my cousin what had happened, but I just couldn't. We didn't have a telephone for me to call my best friend. So, I had to keep everything inside. I didn't know anything about praying to get comfort. I went to church every Sunday, but I had a limited understanding of taking my problems to the Lord. I had too much pride to apologize for my mistake. I should not have sent someone to do what I could have done myself. I didn't think Bob would lie. So, I believed him instead of believing Reuben. To my knowledge, he had never lied to me before. We had never had a big misunderstanding before.

He was always nice and understanding about everything. Whatever I wanted him to do, he did it. Whatever he wanted me to do that didn't get me in trouble, I would do. I knew not to go too far with my desires. Whenever he asked me to do something too far, I could see my dad face and hear his voice in my mind.

You talk about the fear of God; I had a fear of dad. My cousin and her husband were good to me. If I didn't come home until almost dark, they didn't fuss at me. My mom trusted me. I couldn't have faced her if I came up pregnant. I had too many people in my corner. I also wanted to come back to my cousin's house again. The evening was coming to an end. I had to make some decisions. I had never had to decide like this before. I didn't handle my situation in the right way. I jumped to conclusions. That was the wrong thing to do. I didn't know if my friend was going back to the dance or not, but I wanted to go. I wanted to make things right.

I asked my cousin if I could go to the dance. She said, "Alright, remember to be careful and don't do anything you shouldn't be doing." I didn't tell her about my fight with Reuben. I got dressed and walked back to school alone. It was daylight. My friend and I were sitting together, talking, and another young man came over to speak to us. I told her what happened between Reuben and me. I was still angry!

Reuben came over to our table and tried to talk to me. I wouldn't speak to him. He finally left and went outside. My friend and the other young man went outside too. That is when the trouble began. Reuben frightened the young man, so he left and wouldn't talk to me anymore. I finally decided to go home. Reuben walked me home, but it was not a pleasant experience.

The next week was graduation day. Reuben walked out of the schoolyard with another girl. I didn't go after him. The night after graduation, it was another school dance. I was with another young man. Reuben wanted me to come with him, and I wouldn't. He was furious. My date became afraid of Reuben because of the threats Reuben made. My date ran and left me at the dance. The next day was the last day of school, and that was the last day of our relationship. I went home for the summer. He wrote me one letter and came to see me one time. Our relationship was never the same. That's when I found out how much love hurt. It took me a long time to get over that experience.

The next year dad moved closer to town, and I had to go to another high school. I always desired to go to Home Junior School. I heard about this school from my brother and sister, but it didn't live up to its reputation. I had no interest in the school at all. I wanted to go back to the other school. I had to leave all my friends and attend a new school. Reuben was in his senior year. My thoughts were, we might get back together if we saw each other every day.

That summer was hard work in the fields as always. I didn't have anything to look forward to for the summer. I helped mother all I could to keep myself busy. Just before summer ended, our house caught fire and burned to the ground. We lost everything. My dad, mom, niece, and I left the field to eat dinner at noon. After we finished eating, we went to the back of the house in the field. We left my niece to take a nap. Once she woke, she was supposed to come outside to the field. She could see us in the field from the house. She was about four or five years old.

When she wakes up this time instead of coming to the field, she found the matches. Dad left a book of matches behind the bed where he smoked his cigarettes. She set the bed on fire. Thank God she had sense enough to leave the house before the fire spread. While working in the field, we looked back at the house and saw smoke. We ran to the house and tried to put out the fire, but it was too late. It spread all over the place. We didn't have a water hose. We had to draw water from the well and carry buckets to the house. We just couldn't put out the fire. We had nothing left. We lost many of my grandparents' keepsakes. Losing everything was hard on all of us. We had to find somewhere to live. We had no clothes. Only what we had on our backs, I had nothing to wear. It was almost time to start school, but I couldn't begin until two weeks after school started. It was extremely hard for me to catch-up. I had to help finish picking cotton. Mom tried to put together an outfit for me to wear from the things people had given us.

My dad didn't care about mom and me or what we were going to wear. If he got a dollar, he put it on himself. I told my mom; this is my last year going to school. I was tired of looking and dressing worse than anyone else. I had one pair of white oxford shoes someone had given me. I wore those shoes all winter to church and school. The shoes wore out before the end of the school year. The soles of my shoes were flopping, and the children laughed at me. I got a piece of wire and put a small hole in the toe of my shoe. I tied the wire together to stop the flopping. That lasted a while. Then the shoes start to flop again. The sole broke off. My socks were on the ground. I said no more. I can't do this anymore. Mother would have let me wear her shoes, but her feet were so much smaller than mine. She couldn't help me, and dad wouldn't help me.

My cousin, on my mom's side of the family, married a man in the Army. She had a car. She came to visit and sometimes spent the night for a few days. She did this often. My dad thought she was cool. On one of her trips to visit, she brought her boyfriend. My dad knew she was married, but he did not say anything. Dad liked her. I think she was slipping him something to drink. He didn't let me know he drank, but I had heard about it. The next time she came out, she brought her boyfriend's nephew to meet me. I thought if I could be like her, I would be free. I could buy some clothes and do what I wanted to do. I wouldn't have to go to the field anymore. I would have my own money. I wanted to be like my mom's cousin. We have to be careful about how we live our lives and not lead someone in the wrong direction. Children imitate adults and want to be like them. I knew she was doing wrong, but I only saw the part I wanted to. She was free. She was cheating on her husband, and everyone knew it. I solely focused on the material things she acquired. She had a car and her own money. She received her husband's allotment check.

Her nephew became my husband. He was a twenty-year-old short man. I never did like short men, but I settled for him to get out of the field and get some shoes. I was turning sixteen in a month. We met on the 5th of May and got married on the 26th of June 1943. It was crazy. I did not know at the time that he didn't believe in giving women money. He had a job at the defense plant, where they manufactured bombs for war. I thought to myself. This is my ticket out of the fields. I will have money, I can buy shoes, and I will live in town. He asked me to marry him. I said, yes. Then he asked my dad for my hand in marriage, and he said yes. I told mom I was getting married. Mom and cousin got me fixed up for the big day. We got married on my folks' front porch. My cousin made sure I had a few clothes to take with me. I packed my little paper bag and said goodbye with a smile. I didn't know what I was getting myself into, but I soon found out. Things went well for a short while. Then we moved in with his cousin. The fellows went to work every day, and my cousin and I rode around town and spent her husband's allotment check. I was having a good time.

My grandma always said all good things come to an end. She was right. My mom tried to tell me not to marry that boy because she knew I didn't love him. She said it is not going to last. Mom knew how I felt about Reuben. She knew I loved him. A couple of weeks after I got married, mom gave me a letter Reuben wrote to me. I cried as I read the letter, I knew I had made a mistake, but it was too late. I had to try to make the best out of my marriage. Three months after I got married, my husband, uncle, and cousin took the Army's physical examination. Before my husband received his exam, he quit his job. He did not pass the Army's physical because of his eyesight. The other fellows passed.

We visited my husband's family at my mother-in-law's house. We pulled up to his family's home when I noticed eight children peeping at me. They did not have glass windows. They had shutters. They were open to enjoy the nice warm weather. The wooden front doors unhooked and swung outside. I thought, what have I done? What have I gotten myself into this time?

We got out of my cousin's car. My mother-in-law came out to meet me. She was friendly. I went inside the house and sat down. His brothers and sisters were all around me. I was not accustomed to being around a lot of small children. I realized I was going to have to adjust to being around someone younger than me. The children's ages ranged from one to sixteen years old. I said to my cousin in a low whisper. I am ready to go. I thought my husband was going back to work at the shell plant, but he had no intention of going back to work.

We went back to town where we were living with my cousin. Then life changed for me big time. My cousin's boyfriend was deployed. Someone wrote and told her husband that she had an affair. Her husband came home, took the money, car, house, and went back to camp. She had to move back in with her sister. Now, we had no place to live. We always thought it was her sister that told her husband about the affair.

I thought I would be getting an allotment check and living in town. I could buy what I wanted to buy, but no such luck. My husband no longer had a job; he didn't even try to get his old job back. We moved with his mom in the rural part of Louisiana. She had too many people living with her. I was pregnant and couldn't get a job working in the boss's house.

Life had changed, not for the better, but the worse.

We had no money. We moved to the big town of Athens, Louisiana. You could drive through the city while you were looking for it. It had fifty residents, all living about a half a mile apart. I thought I learned what hard times were when I was living with my dad. But I never realized how much more challenging times would be. We lived in a four-room house. We opened the shutters every morning to keep the cold air from coming in through the windows. There was little furniture, an iron bed, two chairs, a homemade table, and a kerosene lamp. We used cardboard boxes to store our clothes.

We covered the box with A clothes item to keep out the dust. We lived beside a dusty dirt road. No one traveled the road unless they were white, owned cars, and the mailman. We could see the sunrise through the wall. When the house was built, the planks were not put close together, or the wood was green when it dried, it left wide spaces between the planks. It was not too bad in the summer, but we almost froze in the winter. We made a temporary fix by pasting newspaper on the walls to keep the wind out. We took papers from the boss' house, and brought it home, laid it on the floor. We cooked flour and water to make a paste and spread it on the back of the paper and paste it against the wall. When the wind blew harshly, it blew the paper off the wall. This would leave a large spot of flour on the wall. Then, we repeated the process all over again. The kitchen was a table to prepare the food and wash the dishes, a four-legged wood-burning stove. There was another long table and homemade bench to sit and eat. Everyone could not sit at the table because it was too many of us. There was not a nearby well to get water. We had to go down a hill and pack water from a spring and carry it back up the hill. The spring water sprung up out of the ground always, both winter and summer. The water was so pleasant and cold in the summer. The best water you ever tasted. We had to go to the well for every use of water: drink, cooking, bathing, and washing.

As you walked across the floor, you could see the ground because the planks were placed far apart. We had nothing to cover the large holes. We had not been introduced to rugs. There were many cold days and nights inside of this house. We had a fireplace, but you couldn't use it because it caught fire and burnt some of the house's insides. It could not be used anymore. We had a four-legged potbelly heater sitting in the middle of the floor. My first child was trying to keep warm, and he burnt his behind. My father-in-law was not a handyman. He didn't fix anything. When it rained, the house was saturated with water from the stovepipes that were not installed correctly in the roof. We had a tin top on the top of the house, and everywhere there was a nail put in to hold the lid on the water would come through. We had buckets all around the inside of the house when it rained. We had very little food to eat for all of us that lived in this house. The family did not have a farm. So, crops were not planted and harvested, nor no animals to slaughter. My father-in-law drove a puck wood truck to haul logs to the sawmill. They made paper and other items from the wood. He drove for a while, and when he got tired of driving and handling logs, he went to the next town to fixed cars. He was good at what he did. He didn't want to work all of the time. He was a little lazy. He didn't try too hard to provide for his family. Most of the time, dad came home on Saturday nights with a large stick of bologna, a can of lard, which we now call shortening, a piece of cheese, crackers, and sardines. Sometimes he brought a piece of meat to cook for Sunday. My father-in-law left Sunday evenings, going back to town. The food lasted until Monday. Then we were out of food again. It was too many of us for the food to last any length of time. He gave my mother-in-law a little money to pay the local store for the food we had gotten on credit. My husband worked for a man that owned a slaughterhouse. During the winter, they sold cows to the local market. Sometimes my husband brought home a beef heart, or liver, for supper. We had hot biscuits, gravy, and a small piece of meat.

My sister-in-law cleaned the boss' house every morning for twenty-five cents a day. Sometimes I worked, I substituted for my sister-in-law if she was ill. It was not much I could do. I had to take care of a small child. I had gotten to know the people in the community well. They all knew that my father-in-law was not a good provider, and my husband followed in his footstep. I'm not sure if one family in the community liked me or felt sorry for me because I was barefoot and pregnant. When I visited their daughter, which was about my age, they always give me greens, peas, potatoes, and sometimes a chicken. They had a farm. They gave me enough food to last a couple of days. After eating all the food, we had to go back to eating biscuits and homemade gravy. We mostly ate this three times a week.

One of our neighbors from the community often teased my mother-in-law, saying he knew we had biscuit and gravy for breakfast again. He could tell by the color of the smoke that came from the rooftop. He thought it was funny, but I was ashamed. It was usual for me to have various food. Two of my bother-in-laws were teenagers. We crossed the pasture in the back of our house and ran the neighbor's chickens until we caught one. My mother-in-law knew we had stolen the chicken, but she didn't say anything. We brought the chicken home, cleaned it, and prepared a hearty dinner for eleven of us to eat. There were never any leftovers.

My mother-in-law didn't know how to provide for her children. She always borrowed food from the neighbors. She never paid them back. The neighbors called borrowing food, "Thank you buckets." When food was given to us, we always said thank. When they saw us coming, they said, here come those children with that "Thank you bucket." There was a store in the neighborhood about a mile away. We went to the store to get flour, sugar, salt, and beans on credit. My husband and his dad paid the store owner on Mondays.

When I first moved in with my in-laws, I didn't rush to eat. My family always had plenty of food and some leftovers. I was slow to go into the kitchen to eat after dinner was cooked. I didn't know there wasn't going to be anything left. I soon learned quickly.

A few times, I did not get anything to eat. I had to go over to the neighbor's house to eat. I soon learned to grab and snatch food like my in-laws were doing before it was all gone. I had to eat in a hurry if I wanted seconds. Most of the time, I piled my plate up, and someone would snatch some of my food off my plate. One day we had meat for dinner. One of the children took the last piece of meat off the serving platter. One of the other children started crying. He stopped crying, ran around to the other end of the table, punched the child in the stomach, and took the meat.

The children were desperate for food. This was the first time in my life I experienced starvation. My grandparents were good providers. Even my dad did not let us go hungry. He planted more cotton to make money and provide food for us to eat. He knew how to get what he wanted. Mom and I just had to work too hard. It taught me a good work ethic. Mom knew how to gather, prepare, and store food for the cold days that were coming. My mother-in-law did not know how to prepare for her children.

Chapter 9

Life was hard for all black people that lived in the south. Black people had to deal with unfair work wages and inadequate housing. It was hard for black parents to support their families. People were tired of working year after year and never experienced mobility. In 1941 War World II opened doors for many black people. The U.S. drafted our men into the armed service. This allowed jobs to open up jobs for many people. People heard about jobs in the northern and western parts of the United States. There were defense plant openings. The plants manufactured everything needed for the war. People were leaving the south, going to California, Illinois, Ohio, and many other states.

Some of our relatives left the south by jumping on freight trains headed north. That is how my brother went. They soon found work, wrote letters to tell their loved ones' work was available. When they earned enough money, they purchased train tickets. The soldiers sometimes sent their family members a ticket to escape the south and the cotton field as well. In those days, people did not forget what they experienced. They helped one another by affording them a better opportunity in life.

Even in the south, some defense plants were opening. All employees did not get equal pay. The difference was so widespread. The people that stayed and worked in those plants did make a profit. They were people that lived in town. The people that lived in the southern states in rural areas were in bondage. The west shipyards built and repaired ships. This was the beginning of the industrial boom for our people.

It was hard to purchase food and clothing items during WWII. The government shipped food and clothes overseas to the soldiers. There were certain materials you could only buy on certain days. The government made stamps to purchase specific items such as sugar, stockings, shoes, and gas. The government established rules to rationed out food, stockings, gas, and shoes. People in the city were affected more because they could not grow their food. The people in the rural areas had an advantage over the people who lived in the city because they grew their food. Growing their crops was a benefit for them because they did not have the money to buy food.

Some of the people on the farm gave food to their relatives or sold their stamps to others. There was always a way to help someone else because everyone was issued stamps. A lot of people didn't have money to purchase the items that were on the stamps. You could see long lines on certain days in front of the stores. If you did not use your stamps on the date issued, they expired. My cousin shared the good news and sent my mom, niece, and nephew train tickets Richard, California. She got a job working in the shipyard right away. It was a chain reaction; people were leaving the south right and left. They were getting away from the $0.50 a day jobs.

Sometimes mom checks were $500 or $600 a week working overtime on the shipyard. Our people had never earned that amount of money in a week. The people thought they were rich. Some of the older people could not make up their minds to go.

My mom lived in California for two months before sending for my dad. She found housing. My mom left six months after I got married. I had to stay behind. Mom said I was too far along in my pregnancy. I might lose the baby. The train ride was six-days.

When my first child was born, I moved into my parents' vacant house. This gave them time to decide what to do about moving their furniture out of the house. The boss began to worry about who was going to work in their fields. My dad told the man that he would be back as soon as the war was over. In a few months, dad and mom bought a house. They had no intention of coming back to Louisiana. Most of my close relatives had left the south. My first cousin was waiting for her husband to send for her. She stayed with me until my baby was born.

She took care of me and my first-born son Alvin. She did everything for me. I only had to take care of the baby. She taught me how to do everything. In those days, we weren't allowed to do very much unless there was no help. My mom sent my husband a ticket. He had to leave me. I was pregnant with my second child and couldn't travel. I cried day and night. Everyone had left me. My husband stayed for a few months and came back to take care of me.

While my husband was away in California, I would go to my distant cousin's house and spend the night. When I had my first child, they wouldn't let me look out the window. They kept the shades closed. The baby didn't open his eyes for a few days.

My mom's older sister died. Dad and mom came back for the funeral. Before they went back to California, they decided to sell the furniture. I didn't have any place to put the furniture because we were going back to my in-law's house.

I was almost ready to go into labor. Since I had given birth to one child, I knew the signs. Mom wanted to stay and be with me when I went into labor early that morning. So, they delayed leaving for a day. The next morning, I got up, made breakfast for the family, and worked in the garden. Dad said, "That girl is not going to deliver that baby now. We have to get back to work." They left the next day. They were half-way home when I delivered my second son. My sister named my son Gaines. That was her friend's name, who finally became her husband. He was born June 8, 1945. My first son was born on March 19, 1944. I had a real hard time trying to work in the field with two babies. My sister stayed with me for a while. She and her friend were having problems. She was living in Houston, Texas. She came to visit before dad and mom left. I had the support to help with my babies. I enjoyed the time we spent together. She taught me how to play cards. We sit up late at night playing cards. She taught me how to play bid whist; it was so much fun. We woke up in the morning, cooked breakfast, and push the dishes to the side and play until it was time to cook dinner.

My sister wrote a letter to her friend, and he wrote her back with money asking her to please come back home. She left without packing her clothes. She said she would get them later. She caught the next bus back to Houston.

After everything was sold, we moved out of the house. My husband had gone back to work for that same man he had worked for before farming. He planted a lot of cottons, and he knew it was no one to help me chop it down. My in-laws had moved out of their house into a new home. We were now living in a house alone. I had to carry the children over to my in-laws before going to the field. They lived about a mile from us. After working in the field all day, I had to walk to my in-law's house to get the babies. Then I had to cook and feed the family, give everybody baths, and get ready for bed.

I had to use a hoe to chop all the grass away from the cotton. When summer was almost over, I had to pick all that cotton. I could not gather as much as my mom when she and I had worked together. She picked 500 pounds a day. I worked right beside her, and I could not pick half that much. Dad always said, you could not sit on her sack because it would hurt your behind. He said she had cotton burs, stalked, and everything else.

The weather was hot. The sack was long with a strap that fits around the neck and across one shoulder. I cried while picking cotton because everybody I loved left and was living a good life. All of my cousins' that I grew up with, and most of my friends no longer lived in Louisiana. I received letters from them telling me how good things were. I waited to receive letters in the mail. They were making money, living in better houses, and no more picking cotton. They didn't even have to say, yes sir anymore unless they wanted too. Grown folks could be grown. Grown men once were called boys, were now called men.

Some men left the state without telling the boss because they knew their boss wouldn't let them go. Some relatives sent enough money to pay the man what they said they owed them. People didn't want their relatives to suffer or get harassed for what they owed the man. Some were afraid to leave, and they just stayed there after the war ended. After 1945 a lot of families never came back, not even to visit for many years. I longed to go west where my folks were. Now I see young women with their children having such a hard time. When they are pregnant, so many things, they can't do. The older folks always said the more active you were, the easier the childbirth would be. When I was pregnant with my first child, I had a taste for chicken and dressing the day before he was born. There was no one home except me. My cousin had gone to town, and my husband was at work. I went outside to catch and kill a chicken. I was going to cook a good meal for Sunday dinner. I started chasing the chicken, and she ran all over the yard. I got so tired, but I was determined to catch her. That chicken ran under the house to the fireplace. With my pregnant stomach, I went all the way under the house and pulled her out. I killed and dressed her and got her ready for cooking. I went to the garden and picked some greens. Saturday, I cooked chicken, dressing, greens, and made a cake. I didn't eat what I cooked. I ate some leftovers and went to bed intending to eat a good dinner, but I worked extremely hard.

My husband came home and didn't eat anything. He took a bath and went to bed. My cousin came home at midnight, drunk. She laid down. After everyone was sound asleep, my labor pains started. For a while, I didn't say anything. I watch the clock to see how close the labor pains were. Finally, I called my cousin. I told her I was having labor pains. She didn't want to wake up. I called her again. She and my husband got out of bed. They set up a while and watched me. I didn't know what to expect. I was a little frightened. Women gave birth at home unless it was a matter of life or death. My husband had to walk about a mile to a friend's house that had a car. He asked for a ride to go into town and pick up the midwife; she was the one that was going to deliver the baby. She is the same midwife who delivered me when I was born. She was my mother's midwife. I trusted her; she delivered both of my boys. When they returned from town, Aunt Topsy examined me. She said you are not ready to deliver yet. She got in her comfortable chair and went to sleep. My cousin and my husband had gone back to sleep, as well. They sat around, ate, and talked in the kitchen. They told me if I eat anything while in labor, I will have a greedy baby, so I didn't eat. I thought this would all be over by dinner. Then I can eat what I cooked.

My baby was born at 6:30 pm Sunday. I thought now I can eat. They brought me a biscuit and a cup of coffee. The old folks would not give you particular foods after childbirth. I was so disappointed. I worked hard to fix that food and only got to smell it. Both boys were born in Louisiana.

Well, now I finally get my chance to go to California. In December of 1946, mom sent my family train tickets so we could live with them. I packed all our stuff in three boxes. We didn't have much. I had one decent dress, and I wore that on the train. I had one pair of shoes, brown oxfords. The children had a few clothes. We all wore our best clothes. This was my first time being on a train. I had only been on a local bus. I had to stand on the bus when I went into town. There were only two rows of seats in the back for us to sit. When those seats were filled, we had to stand. The other seats were for white folks. If the white folks' section became full, we had to give up our seats so they could sit down.

The train ride took five days from Louisiana to California. I was afraid of being around people that I didn't know. I had never been in a public restroom, only when we went to town, in that nasty little place set aside for us to use. You couldn't lock the doors. I had two babies that needed to be changed, and I waited as long as I could before asking where the restroom is.

We exchanged trains when we arrived in Kansas City. I took my oldest child to the restroom to clean him up. I saw the restroom doors. I didn't have any change, because I didn't have any money. I waited around the restrooms until everyone left. I got down on my knees and pushed my son under the door. Then I crawled under the door. When I finished, I waited until everyone left out the restroom, and we got on the floor and crawled back out. I later found out there was one stall opened.

I was so green. I had never been anywhere before. My dad told a hilarious story about one of our relatives. Right before they arrived at the next train stop, the porter went down the aisle and called out the next town approaching. Our cousin was in the restroom when the porter said Crocket. He thought the man said lock it. He ran out of the restroom before he pulled up his clothes. He thought they were going to lock the bathroom.

I think about how unknowledgeable I was to crawl under the restroom door. I didn't have enough sense to turn the knob and walk out. We made another stop, and my husband got off the train to find something cheap for the babies to eat. After he got off the train, the train switched tracks. He had his tickets in his pocket. I thought they were going to put us off the train. I started crying. I thought they were leaving him, but he knew they had switched, and he came back. That was my first and last train ride. I thought, oh, how good life is going to be for my family and me. We lived with my parents in their two-story house. My dad rented rooms on the second floor. The two-bedroom downstairs was for my parents and my little niece. We had to sleep in the breakfast room in a twin bed. Dad thought that was enough for us because he did not expect us to stay very long. Dad kept asking when our clothes were going to arrive. He was tired of seeing us wear the same clothes over and over. What he didn't know is that we didn't have any nice clothes in the boxes. We found out later when we changed trains. Our clothes didn't change the train with us. We waited two weeks before we were notified to come to pick up our boxes. Some of my cousins lived near my dad. They went to the store to purchase some things for us. Dad didn't offer to buy us anything.

We took the bed's mattress and put it on the floor for the boys. They were one and two years old. My husband and I slept on the box spring. We ate with the family for about two weeks. Then my dad told mom to let us feed ourselves. The war had ended, and jobs were hard to find. My husband was looking for a job every day. We had no money to buy food. Mom slipped and gave me food. They found a church home, and every Sunday, they were bringing home company. I helped serve the table so we could have a few leftovers to eat. The company asked dad, Brother Motherland, who is this young lady, and dad replied, oh, that's my daughter. He was ashamed of me. I was ashamed of myself, but I couldn't do any better at the time.

If I had doubts about how dad felt about me, I soon found out. Nothing had changed. I couldn't go to church because I didn't have proper clothes for the boys and me. I always stayed at home and had dinner ready when they came home. My dad was not fond of banks, so he loaned money out to the roomers and relatives. They had to pay him back as soon as possible. He told everybody what he had done. He wanted a large house to make money. As soon as one renter moved out, he put that sign in the window to fill the room again more quickly. He didn't even share the rent money with mom.

I never thought my dad would have treated me as he did. I knew he was selfish, but I didn't realize his selfishness was that bad. He was all about money for himself. Mom was as sweet as could be, but she was a little afraid of dad. Dad went to town and bought her something nice on credit. Then he gave her the bill. She had to work and pay for whatever he picked out.

Dad and mom were always big churchgoers. He attended church dressed to kill. He loved quality clothes, and he loved to go to church and flash cash. He always tried to put more in the offering than anyone else. When some relatives came around wearing new clothes, dad felt the material to see if he approved of the material. He didn't wear cheap clothes. Whatever mother got, she put it in layaway and paid for it out of her housework pay.

Dad and my husband were two people I had to pray hard, not to hate. I finally got over the way they treated me. At one time, it was hard for me to talk about my experience with them without crying. Now I can with the help of the Lord.

Chapter 10

My brother came home from the army. He didn't go back to Louisiana. He divorces his wife and daughter. He married another young lady from New Orleans. His wife had a brother that lived in one of dad's rented rooms. He noticed that we were not eating with the family every evening. He told me he would give me ten dollars a week to buy and cook dinner for him. He also offered us his leftovers.

Ten dollars bought enough for us. I learned the hard way to survive on $10 for my family. The leftovers were for my husband, myself, and my two baby boys. This is how we survived until my husband found a job. Sometimes I walked over to my cousin's house. She fixed us dinner. In the first year of my marriage, I weighed ninety-five pounds. I didn't eat enough food to get fat. I never weighed over 135 pounds. When I was pregnant with my two boys, I lost weight as soon as they were born.

My husband found employment at a flower shop in

Oakland, California. He rode the bus to work. I found a job as a housekeeper. Mom referred me for the job. Her employer gave her a lead to the job. The lady was nice enough to let me bring my boys to work. The job was within walking distance from where we lived. We saved enough money to rent an apartment. We bought and cooked our food. Sometimes I brought home food from work as well. My dad bought a television for the living room. He did not let my boys come into the living room to watch the television. The boys had to sit on the steps and look through the bars of the stairs. I was allowed to clean the room and the television, but I couldn't turn it on. He only allowed my niece to turn on the television and play the recorder. That made me feel as if I was not good enough, or maybe he thought I didn't know how to operate the television. My oldest son has vague memories of this experience. I sat on the steps with them, so they didn't feel bad.

My husband's uncle lived in the same town. His uncle went to Louisiana to visit. While he was there, his sister told him we were living in California. She gave him our address, and she wrote a letter to us and gave us his address. We caught the bus to visit his uncle and aunt. They told us about an apartment that was near there house. We went to see the apartment and talk to the landlord. After talking with the landlord, she rented us the apartment.

Our landlord was a real estate investor. She owned lots of property. She had one daughter. Her daughter was grown, married, and had her own family. She and her mom had some issues. Her mom and husband drank heavily and did not go to church. The daughter was a mild Christian young lady. The landlord and her husband's office were downtown. They stayed busy. They were involved in so many civic affairs. They were always on the go. After she got to know me, she sometimes stopped by and asked if I would clean her house?
She was preparing to host a big party.

She sometimes had piles of clothes on her bed that she did not take time to hang up in the closet. She gave me four or five dresses for hanging the clothes and cleaning the room. She also gave me clothes for my boys. I didn't realize then, but I know now that was God's hand at work.

I could not afford to buy clothes for myself or my boys. I never did like to see a mother all decked out, and her children looking ran down. I would rather go without clothes. I enjoyed making a home for my husband and boys. Coming from Louisiana's fields to Richmond, California, was a big adjustment for me.

I spent time at home, cooking, cleaning, and taking care of my family. I loved trying new cookie recipes for the boys and their friends. The boys sometimes went out to play and brought their friends inside for cookies and milk. I learned how to starch and iron clothes at an early age. I starched and ironed my children's blue jeans and shirts. They looked so handsome. They only had a few clothes at the time, but I kept them cleaned, starched, and ironed. I also starched and ironed my husband's khaki pants and shirts.

Mom taught me to wash and iron when I was at home. I learned because I sometimes made $0.50 or $0.75, washing and ironing for the boss before leaving Louisiana. I went to the big house to wash their clothes, but I couldn't iron their clothes up there. They brought the clothes to my house to iron. One day I went to the big house to wash, and it started raining while I was washing. I pulled the tub of clothes under the hangover on the house's side to avoid getting wet. The nice lady was preparing a birthday dinner for her father-in-law. When they finished eating, she brought me a plate of food. It was raining so hard it was popping the peas out of the plate. I had to eat outside, pressed up against the house wall. This prevented all the food from being washed out of my plate. I thought to myself, I clean the house, but can't eat inside, not even in the kitchen? I can say through it all the Lord brought me from a mighty long way.

Our finances were getting better, and life was looking brighter. My husband became abusive. I found another job, and he started a fight about income. He could neither read nor write. I tried to help him by encouraging him to start night school, and I would go with him. He wouldn't accept my help. Everything I tried to do failed. He was always suspicious of others.

If I went to the store to purchase items for dinner or get school supplies for the boys, he would accuse me of giving my money to another man. That is when he physically abused me. He felt like he had to teach me a lesson. The abuse became so bad I had to carry a pen and paper to write all my items down to let him know how much money I spent. Once I got home, I sat down with him to go over the itemized list. After explaining the line item by line item, he still didn't believe me. His job ended, and things got tight again.

I met another couple that was renting from the same landlord. We became acquainted. Their names were John and Ann; they were a young couple. They were from Texas. They got married and moved to California. John was a veteran, and with his housing benefits, he was eligible for adequate housing. We found an apartment and moved in together. Things got better while living with John and Ann until my husband started to become physically abusive again. When he wanted to fight me, he would take me in the car and go to some deserted place and do his dirty work. I would cry. After a while, he stopped taking me away, and he just closed the bedroom door and whipped me and dared me to say anything when I came out of the room. He told me he would kill me if I ever called the police on him, and I thought he would, I was just that afraid of him.

Summer of 1947, my husband got a new job in the state of Washington. He and my cousin visited Washington to see about a job. They got hired for the job. They lived in Washington until they saved enough money to return to California and moved us to Washington. Myself, the two boys, and my cousin's wife. My cousin found housing in Pasco, Washington, and my husband found housing in Yakima, Washington. That was an eighty miles drive. I didn't know anyone in the neighborhood just in case I had to reach out for help.

The physical abuse in my marriage became more frequent. My husband became friends with his co-workers. I finally met a lady, and she was friendly. My husband didn't like her. He didn't want me to befriend her because she didn't have a husband. I was not allowed to visit her when he was at home. She saw marks on me and asked, what are those scars? I lied and told her I fell, but she didn't believe me, so she asked me one day, why do you allow that little man to whip on you all of the time? I replied, I am afraid of him.

I worked next door to our home. The boys stayed with a neighbor while I worked. I had no money to buy stamps. I wasn't allowed to spend any of my paychecks. One morning I headed out to go to work. My husband was at home around 7:00 am. I heard a fire truck. I looked out the window and saw the flames coming from our house. We lived with a single lady, and she was in bed, sleeping. When I left for work, my husband was cooking breakfast for the boys. My oldest son had awakened. He found the matches on the table by the bed. My husband smoked in bed, and he left the matches and cigarettes by the bed. My son saw the matches and was playing with them and set the bed on fire.

My husband smelled smoke and went to check on the boys. He awakened the lady and barely had time to snatch the boys out of bed. He said the oldest was awoke, but he was afraid to get up. The fire engulfed the bed. My baby boy was still asleep. We lost everything. I felt so bad because of the lady's loss, and it was Christmas season. She rented us a room, and she lost everything. We all had to start over. We found a house around the corner from where we were living. The landlady found another place. People gave us furniture and clothes. I thought this was going to be a sad Christmas for the boys. Someone recommended us to the Salvation Army. They bought food and one toy each for the boys, and a little gift for the adults. I did not let mom know what was going on, because I knew she would worry. When I see the Salvation Army on the streets now, I feel the need to help them, because they helped me. I love helping people.

Jobs were not as high in demand, and the job market was changing. My husband and cousin were laid off. We stayed where we were living until the summer. The weather was scorching hot. I remember one hot summer day. My husband left the house like he usually did. I cleaned the boys up and went outside to sit under the shade tree with my neighbor. My husband had a green 1935 Ford. I saw the car coming around the corner. I got a sick feeling in my stomach. I knew what was coming. He drove the car up in the driveway, got out, and went inside. Then he came back to the door and called me inside. He asked me why was I outdoors? I told him it is hot inside. We had no fan and had never heard of air condition. He slapped me upside my head and told me to keep my you know what in the house. He got back in his car and left.

My neighbor came into the house and asked, why didn't I come back outside? I was sitting in the house, sweating, and crying. She asked, "Did he hit you?" I said yes, and I am afraid he will come back and do it again if I come outside. She said, "I hope you burn up in here." She said she would not let a man do that to her, but she wasn't aware of how afraid I was of him.

My neighbor encouraged me to write a letter to my cousin to let her know how my husband treated me. If I was not going to do anything about it, let someone know what was going on. I wrote the letter and told them what a fearful time I was having. They quickly moved to Pasco. We moved into the apartment with them. I found work at the local hospital. My husband was not able to find a job. Despite our living arrangements and being unemployed, he took me in the car and drove to a secluded place to beat me. The boys were too afraid to tell. The boys were ready to start school.

I homeschooled the boys. It was fun getting them ready for school. During that time, I worked at the Catholic

Hospital. The mother of the hospital and I had the same name, Mildred. The nurses called me Millie. Some people still call me Millie. I like that job. I resigned from the position because my cousin wanted to go back to California.

In October of 1950, we packed our bags and moved back to California. I moved back in with my dad for a short while. We soon found work and moved out. I went back to my previous landlord, where I lived before. I had promised the boys a television. I told dad I would buy the boys a television. His reply was they don't need one. I bought it anyway. When dad came to visit, the boys knew how to operate the television. Dad said the children are going to tear up that thing. I felt good because we were in our place. He didn't buy the television, I did.

I was pregnant with my oldest daughter. I was still getting slapped around. On February 23rd, she was born. My friend named her Delores. I tried to stay in the marriage for the sake of the children hoping it would get better. When growing up, I never wanted two or three sets of children by different men. I wanted them all to have the same dad. I made a sacrifice to keep this promise to myself.

About a month before, Dolores was born. One Saturday, my husband came to work with me so that I could get some food. He didn't want to stop to get food when I got off work. He was going out later. I dropped him off at the house. I was driving on a major highway, 65 to 70 miles per hour on my way back home. It was an accident ahead of me. I was in the inside lane when I began to see the taillights ahead. I didn't know the wreck was up ahead. I changed lanes to pass the traffic. When I started down the hill, I saw the crash. I was going too fast to come to a complete stop. When I slammed on my breaks to stop, the car made a full 360-degree turn in the middle of the road three times before coming to a stop. When I came to a complete stop, I didn't hit any other cars. I frighten the officer standing in the street so bad. He just waved his hand for me to go on. I now know that the good Lord was riding with me.

I left the boys at home in the bed asleep. I was trying to get back home before they woke up. The car doors on the driver side latch were broken, and every time you turn the corner, the door swung open. When the car was spinning around, the door did not swing open. That is why I knew the Lord's hand was holding that door closed. My husband never got the door repaired. He knew how to hold the door when he was driving.

Some of my husband's coworkers saw the car spinning while on their way to work. They recognized the car and knew it was me driving. When I saw them after the highway incident, they said they were praying that I would not turnover. I was eight months pregnant. The next week after everything was over. I thought about what could have happened. I became nervous and got the shakes for a while. I was so frightened.

A few weeks after the accident, my baby was born. One of my husband's brothers was in the armed forces, and he was station nearby. He came to visit us at the right time. He took care of me for two weeks. I stayed home and took care of the children until the baby was old enough for me to go back to work. I looked for someone to take care of the children. There was a neighbor that lived across the street in front of us. She was always friendly to the children. She retired from her job. She often asked if she could give the children something, she bought for them. The boys liked her very much. I asked her if she would consider keeping the children so I could look for work. She said she would be glad to watch them for me.

I heard there were some open positions at one of the local hospitals. I applied for the position and got the job. I had always dreamt of becoming a nurse one day. I worked there for a while and was doing fine. I had no car, so I carpooled with a coworker. This went well for a short time, then my husband got jealous and started fighting me because I rode to work with my coworker. I finally left the job.

My friend Ann told me the hospital she was employed at was hiring. She drove me to the hospital, and I applied for the nurse's aide position and was offered the job. I worked closely with nurses and patients. My job duties consist of changing the patient's clothes, feeding patients, taking temperatures, and making beds. The job was a perfect fit for me.

One Sunday morning, Ann and I arrived to work. One of my patients died. The head nurse came in and told us she wanted us to close the patient's eyes, stuff her rear with cotton before they took her to the morgue. I looked at Ann. I said, are you going to do what she asked? Ann said, yes, I am. I said I couldn't do that. I feared the look of blood, but I thought I could get over that. But to work with the dead was too much for me. I knew the dead couldn't hurt me in my heart, but as my grandpa once said, they would make me hurt myself.

I just could not put my hands on the patient after they stopped breathing. I went to the head nurse, told her my fear. I asked her to transfer me to housekeeping. This was the end of my nursing career. Ann did what she was told to do and was promoted to head nurse herself. Our careers parted ways.

Ann and her husband shared a car. She drove the car. He rode to work with his coworker. I continued to ride to work with Ann for the few months I worked at the hospital. We had some things in common. I had two boys, I was from Louisiana, and she was from Texas. We both married young, but her husband did not abuse her. We both moved to different cities. She went on to pursue her nursing career, and

I continued working in housekeeping.

I let fear control my life. I was afraid to take any chances. I coward down in my home life until it affected my whole family. I had no confidence in my ability to do anything. There were so many things I thought I could not do. I didn't grow up like that. Before I married, I tried lots of things to see how it worked. My baby girl right now does not have the confidence she should have in herself. She is brilliant.

When they were growing up, I taught all my children. They can do anything they want to do as long as they set their minds to it. I gave my children good advice, but it was hard for me to take my advice. I hope some young ladies will read this book and learn from my mistakes.

I had three children, a controlling husband, but life didn't stop there. I had to survive for the sake of my children. I had supportive neighbors and friends. Most of all, I had to learn to put my trust in the good Lord above. I had strayed away from my home upbringing, but I had to come back to it.

I learned I couldn't make it on my own.

Chapter 11

Mom encouraged me to start back attending church, and I also needed to get the children into Christian activities. I lived near the church where my mom and dad attended. I could walk to church in five or ten minutes. I followed her advice. I started back attending church, and I joined the choir. I loved to sing, even though I don't think I do an excellent job sometimes. They tell me my birth mother had a good voice. I know my aunt, my mom's sister, had a great voice and sang well. Both of my girls have the gift of singing. It was inherited. After I became active in church, my children were involved in some of the children's church activities. My husband got jealous and decided I couldn't go back to that church so. I left that church.

My husband's uncle and his wife attended another church that was near the house. It was a little further to walk, but I didn't mind walking to minimize physical abuse. I started to participate in the new church. I eventually joined. I thought this would influence my husband to attend church with me. My folks were always Methodist Denomination. This church was Baptist, so I had to be baptized underwater. We encouraged my husband to see me get baptized, but he never set foot in that church. I wanted my family to attend church together. I thought this would bring us closer together, but it did not change a thing. After a while, I went back to my folk's church so the children could get a sense of family; even his uncle and his wife tried to encourage him to come to church. He rode around with his friends and drank.

I always tried to keep peace in the house, but it didn't help at all. I was still abused. I continued to work, catching rides with whomever I could. If the traffic was heavy, and I got home late. Another fight would breakout. If we left the hospital a little later than usual, that would give him a reason to hit me. It didn't matter what the problem was; he punched or slapped me. I was going to be abused, no matter what. I finally had enough. I couldn't take any more abuse. I left and filed for divorce. He moved out of the house. I went to court. My cousin went with me. My husband was a no show. He thought if he didn't show up, I couldn't get the divorce, but I did. My divorce was granted.

I went home, and I was at peace for a while. He visited my relatives' home and begged them to talk to me. I allowed family and friends to persuade me to reconcile my marriage. He promised to do better, but deep down inside, I knew he hadn't changed. For the sake of the children, I went back and tried it again. He put on an excellent front when we were around others. We had been married for eleven years. I wanted to believe he had changed. The children loved their dad. I always told the children, whatever happens, it didn't have anything to do with our love for them, and they should always respect their dad. If I got hit around them, they didn't interfere; my youngest would get help if we were around anyone.

In August of 1955, my husband got a job at another large corporation in Oakland, California. He worked there for a short time, and the plant transferred to Los Angeles. My cousin and I were still traveling together. My husband and her husband were good friends. They ran around together, but he disapproved of the way he treated me. So, we moved again. Maybe this change will bring about more happiness—a new place, new friends, and leaving his old friends behind.

My cousin did not work, so she kept the children while I worked. She had no children, but she was very fond of children. I soon found housework. My husband always told me how stupid I was. He beat all the self-esteem out of me. I had no self-esteem to look for anything better. He could not read, but I was the one stupid. I was not stupid. I was controlled by fear.

The men started working and found housing. This time my cousin would not let him move me by myself. We moved into an upstairs apartment. I told my husband I would not be running from him up and down the stairs and take a chance on breaking my legs anymore. The abuse continued. The apartment we moved into was too small for our family. We needed an additional room. It was not long before one of my husband's brothers came to live with us. We had three children and three adults that was too many people for a small one-bedroom apartment. I looked for a larger apartment. We paid our rent by the week. Every Saturday morning, the manager came to collect the rent for the week. When my husband was not home, I asked the manager if he had a larger vacant apartment available. If my husband knew I was asking for a larger place, he would have been angry. He didn't want to pay any more than what he was paying. We were spending thirteen dollars a week. To him, that was enough crowded or not. Finally, the manager told me he had a vacancy to meet our needs. This place was fifteen dollars a week. I asked if we could rent the apartment, and he said yes. This was a large complex, with buildings on both sides of the street. The place I wanted to move in was across the street from where we were living.

Every time I found out about a larger apartment vacancy; I asked the manager if we could move. Each time it was across the street. One time it was next door to where we lived. The boys joked about us, moving from one side of the street to the other. They told their friends we were moving again. Where are you moving too? The boys said back across the street. Their friends thought they were going to move out of the neighborhood. I enquired about other apartments, but they required you to pay rent by the month, and my husband did not think he could pay rent by the month. That was too much to pay at one time. Before going to work, I woke up early to dress the children for school. If it were the weekend, the children could play after I fed them. I took my baby to my cousin's house across the street before walking to the bus stop. The bus stop was about three blocks away. Sometimes I had to transfer two or three times, depended on how far I had to go.

We lived in South Los Angeles, and the best-paying jobs were on the far west side of town.

I worked for Lillian, and we became friends. We were about the same age. She had three children. She was nice enough to recommend me to her sister and two of her friends for additional work. I worked every day. This gave my husband more reasons to fight. Sometimes I was asked to work night parties. This provided more money for the family and extra food from the party to bring to the children. One night I worked at a party near Beverly Hills. My husband was too evil to let me use the car to drive to work. He wouldn't take me to work or pick me up. I had to catch the bus. I got off work at about 1:00 am. The buses ran slow late at night. I had to ride three buses to get home after I finished work. I stood at the bus stops. Afraid someone would try to harm me.

After getting off the last bus and walking three blocks to my apartment, my husband met me outside the house, asking, where have I been all that time? He accused me of being with another man. I was frightened, cold, crying, and tired. This was the night I decided I was not going to accept another beating.

I went inside the apartment. He attempted to hit me. I pushed past him, went straight to the kitchen, and dropped the food. I snatched open the drawer where I kept my butcher knives and pulled one out of the drawer. I didn't know at the time that my youngest son was watching me when I got the knife. He ran to get my cousin. The children never saw me in that frame of mind. My husband went out of the door. My cousin came to the door. I was ready to hurt him that night. I was not going to be beaten without a fight. My husband wouldn't give me enough money to take care of the children's school needs. I was working to help provide for the family and meet the needs of our children. I refused to allow him to greet me in this manner. Oh no, not tonight. After this was all over and they calmed me down, I just broke down and cried.

He stopped beating me for a long time, and then I allowed him to start again.

When we were fighting, oh, I mean when he was beating me, I didn't know them. That man that was living there at the time is now my husband. When I was allowed to sit on the steps and watch the children play, I never looked at the men as he passed by. I wasn't allowed to look at no other man. When I met him eleven years later, we had both moved to a different location. We met at a church after I divorced. We just happened to talk about where we use to live in the early years. We knew some of the same people when I lived in the apartment complex. One of my old neighbors uses to ride to church with him. I knew her, I knew she went to church, but I didn't know him. Small world, I thought. He even remembered my first husband. When I described him, he said that little man used to take my parking spot. He remembered the color of the old Cadillac he drove. I guess it was not time for us to meet. We went to visit one of our neighbors after we met, and she tried to make me remember who he was, but I didn't remember seeing him. He said he used to take the broom and bang on the ceiling of his apartment for us to stop the noise. While he was at work, his wife was out with other men.

After we moved to Los Angeles, my cousin and I went back to Oakland to worked seasonally at the Fruit Canner. We traveled six hundred miles to work. We did this for a few years. Our husbands looked forward to us leaving. We worked for three months and saved our money to bring home. Our husbands waited for the money so they could trade cars again. I was crazy enough to give the money to my husband. I knew my husband would not let me drive our car unless he felt like it, and that was not too often. On one of my trips back to work, my husbands' brother moved with us in our one-bedroom apartment. His sister from Louisiana moved into our apartment with her husband and three children. I had no idea they were even thinking about coming to visit. When the working season was over, we came home. I was in shock when I walked into my apartment and saw all those folks. No one cleaned the apartment. I had to go to my cousin's apartment and sit down and cry. I kept everything neat and polished. Instead of dusting everything, I washed everything. I was just sick.

My sister-in-law and her family had taken over my bedroom. My two boys and my brother-in-law slept in the living room. My baby girl slept on the living room floor. My husband and I slept on the kitchen floor. People had to step over us at night, to get water from the refrigerator. I had to get up early so my sister-in-law could fix breakfast for her husband and brother before they went to work. When everyone left for work, I could not go back to sleep. There was no place to lay down. This was my apartment; something was wrong with this picture. I had to start looking for another apartment.

My husband gave me $10 a week to buy groceries for my family and brother-in-law. I had to stretch the money to make sure we had enough groceries to last a week. I purchased: three pounds of ground beef for one dollar, three pounds of wieners for one dollar. Five pounds of neckbones for one dollar, five loaves of bread for one dollar, ten pounds of chicken for one dollar, five bunches of mustard and turnip greens for one dollar, and whatever else I could get for the remaining three dollars and fifty cents.

I always saved $0.50 for a taco and a drink night with my cousin and sister-in-law. That was my treat for the week. This was the only time my husband allowed me to drive the car. When we grocery shopped, we went to four stores to purchase sell items from the sales ad papers. The men watched the children until we returned. We had to shop as fast as we could to return the car to the men. They had plans to go out clubbing. The women stayed at home with the children. My husband always started an argument with me about money right before he walked out the door. He knew I had no way to follow him.

It was almost time to celebrate Thanksgiving. This was always exciting for me because I might get another ten dollars for grocery shopping. Most of the time, I had to use the money from my paycheck, which caused me to get another whipping from my husband. My sister-in-law moved into the apartment

I found. We went shopping as we always did, and this time each of us had enough money to buy a turkey. We purchased a turkey to fix for Thanksgiving. When I finished putting away my groceries, I went across the street to check on her. I knew she was not used to city apartment living. I walked into her apartment, and I asked her how she was doing? I then asked, "Do you have everything put away?" She said yes. I asked, are you going to stuff the turkey or not? She replied, "My turkey is in the oven. I asked, "Have you cleaned the turkey?" She replied, "The rapper said, ready to cook." She put the turkey in the oven with the plastic wrapper on it. We had to take it out of the oven, cool it down, remove the wrapper, and wash it. That's how country some of us were when we came to the city.

My husband's brother was still living with us. He met a young lady in the complex and wanted to marry her. I hurried and found an apartment for him. He gave me the money to cook for the wedding. I made the wedding cake, fixed all the food for the wedding. They wanted to get married Saturday morning, but everything was closed. He let me know what had happened, but I had already prepared everything. They didn't even tell her mother because they were supposed to go back the next week to get the blood test and other arrangements, but they never did. They went on to have three children. We had the reception, everyone ate, drank, and went home. They moved out of my apartment. I finally had my bedroom back. I could sleep in my bed. Oh, how good that felt.

In October 1959, my youngest baby girl was born. We named her Dietra. My boys were born close together, one year and three months apart. My second son and my oldest daughter have a seven-year difference in age. My daughters are seven years apart. I didn't get whipped while I was pregnant with my children. My husband and cousin stayed out late one night. I slept by the window. I heard the car when they drove up. I got up and looked out the window. My cousin came up the stairs, but my husband got out of my cousin's car, got into our car, and drove off. I was in my third trimester. My relatives told him to stop taking the car because someone might have to take me to the hospital. He came and stole the car and didn't come back until 3:00 pm the next day. I was standing on the steps, waiting for him when he started up the steps. I stepped in front of him; I knew he would not hit me in front of all the people standing outside. I cursed him badly, even though I would get it after my baby was born. I let out all my anger. I learned he took another woman to San Diego for the night.

I continued to do housework while my cousin took care of the children. I learned my way around Hollywood and Beverly Hills on the bus. My cousin let me use his car when my employer's house was not within walking distance from the bus stop. Sometimes they lived way up in the Hills. My cousin carpooled with my husband since they worked together. I could use my cousin's car, but I couldn't use our car. Something was wrong with that picture.

We finally moved out of the apartment to another part of town. All of my relatives and friends were moving out. My sister was going from one house to another, living with relatives. I asked her to come live with me. She slept all day. This was too much strain on me and the children. The lifestyle she was living was not the example I wanted my girls to see. She moved out and went back to Oakland.

I had found housing for everyone else. Now I could live in peace. We took a trip to Louisiana and brought my younger sister-in-law back to California to live with us. I wanted her to have a better life. She lived with us for a few years. She got a job at a department store; she was doing well. She was one year older than my oldest son. She was like a daughter to me. She sang in the church choir and met a young man. After dating for a while, she became pregnant. He didn't go to our church. I asked her about the young man and what were they going to do? She said they were not going to get married. My children told me the young man was already married. I talked to her about the situation. Her oldest sister offered her to come to live with her. They wanted to appear as if I was mean. I was not. I just wanted him to do what was right.

We graduated from apartment living and moved to a duplex. One of my brother-in-law's lived on the other side of the duplex. He met a lady that lived in the complex and married her. Everyone was trying to do better. My youngest daughter started school. I moved away from my cousin, so I no longer had a babysitter for my daughter. I had to arrange my work schedule around her new school. Sometimes I had to take her to work with me. It was a blessing to see my oldest son graduate from high school. My boys were a grade difference in school. With my youngest he was not as serious about school as my oldest son. He ran with the wrong crowd skipping school, riding around town, going to schools where he wasn't enrolled. I received so many calls and notes from teachers until they put him in an alternative school. He changed his behavior because he didn't want to be there. He wanted to go back to regular high school. After completing the alternative school, he returned to his regularly assigned high school and graduated. I met a neighbor that didn't work. She kept my daughter for me after school until I returned home from work. That made things better for me. My home life was still abusive. I tried to stay until everyone finished school, but I couldn't take another day.

Mildred & her brother A.J. Moreland

1984

Chapter 12

My cousin and husband loved to play cards. They started playing when they came home from work. They moved the card game to the inside of the house and continued to play all night. The only time they stopped was to eat supper. Then they started all over again. We met another couple that enjoyed playing. We started having card parties at each other's homes. We served cake and coffee. It finally turned into full cooked meals. The men had their juice. When the men started losing the card game, they switch from playing cards to dominoes.

No one knew I could play rise and fly. I learned to play years ago. When we played, we called next. After we beat all the ladies, then we took on the men. I played so hard, watching those cards. I even played in my sleep. I knew this was getting to me. I decided I played long enough. I stopped playing altogether, and our card-playing buddies moved away. Then, I started attending church again.

In 1957 my dad's sister died in California. Her children shipped her body back to Louisiana. Because one of her sons still lived there. He had ten children, and he could not afford to come to California. We rode with my cousin to Louisiana to attend the funeral. We had no money, and black people weren't allowed to stay in hotels. I wasn't sure where we were going to stay. My other cousin stayed with her brother; so, dad and I left.

My dad and I stayed with my half-sister, my dad's daughter. I had gotten older, and I no longer felt the same about her as in the past. I realized it was not her fault what her mom and my dad did. She made us feel welcomed and waited on dad hand and foot. The trip was nice; it healed a lot of hurt and emotional wounds. While we were there, she gave us her sister's address in San Diego, California. When we returned home, dad wrote me a letter asking me to take him to visit his daughter. Dad traveled from Richmond, Virginia, to Los Angeles, California. My husband, children, and I drove dad to see his daughter. It was a pleasant visit. While in Louisiana, I visited my half-brother by my dad. I learned to forgive others.

Holding on to past hurt, pain, and misery only continued to harm me and stop me from moving forward in life. My brother and I grew up together. My half-brother and biological brother were the same age. My dad was quite a fellow in his day. My half-brother and dad had similar features, and he looked a little like my biological brother.

After the trip to Louisiana, dad became ill. I visited Richmond to see dad. He cried when I brought his food to the bed. He never verbally apologized. I knew he was sorry for the way he treated me. Dad died, December 10, 1963. Dad was ill for quite some time. He smoked heavily for many years. His fingers were brown on the tips of both hands. The doctor said it was tobacco stains and his lungs were like a sifter full of holes.

My dad's illness had worsened. He had worked in a pottery plant for about fifteen years; so, the tobacco and the pottery dust caused him to contract tuberculosis (TB). I had moved from Northern California to Southern California. My niece called to let me know dad was taken to the hospital. They didn't think he would make it this time. As I prepared to drive to Richmond, he was dead when I arrived. Mom was devasted. She always depended on dad to take care of everything. I could never understand that. She was a very self-sufficient person when she met him. Then she stopped taking care of the household responsibilities. She didn't know anything about the bills they owed. I guess it was to keep down problems. She wanted to move back and take over the house. I could not just pull up and move. I had a family, a job, and I needed time.

After the homegoing service, I returned to Southern California. That was the last time I saw mom alive. She had a heart attack and died three months and ten days after dad's death. She had no will to live after dad passed. After mom's service, I got in the car and looked at the window where she and I use to sit and looked out. I thought in my mind. I do not have to prove to mom anymore. I tried hard to make my marriage work. Now it was all over.

It was a matter of time that I filed for divorce again—this time for good. No more going back. This was the end. I wanted to pick the right time to tell my husband. Eventually, he left me no choice. When dad died, he didn't leave us any money. He left us the house. My niece wanted to keep the house. She was young, and her priorities were not in the right place. My sister's daughter refinanced the home, and she paid my brother and me our portion. My sister was not financially able to help her daughter, so she lost the house. She gave away everything mom left behind to people she did not know. She did not call to tell me anything. I told her I was coming back to Louisiana soon. When I went back for a visit, she left and moved out of the house to Berkeley. All of mom's items were gone. I was so sorry I didn't do what mom asked me to do.

I received almost enough money to put a down payment on a house for my family. I needed four hundred dollars to have the down payment on my first dream house. I worked and saved enough money to get the house. I searched for a house. I drove around searching for a home on the days I had a chance to use the car. During the search, I found the house I desired. This house had two bedrooms, a den, a large living room, a large kitchen, one bath, and a service porch. There was a large backyard with fruit trees and grapevine. My brother was a state licensed real estate broker. He came from Oakland to draw up the contract to purchase the house. He told me if I find a house, give him a call, and he will fly in town. He kept his word, and he got the commission. This was the only thing my brother ever did for me. My brother and I didn't grow up together, so I didn't know him. We weren't close at all. Three years before he died, we established a relationship and spent time together and talk about old times and old people. My brother was selfish. He had a good-paying career, and as we say, he made it, but he didn't try to pull anyone else up with him. He bragged about what he had. He often called me to let me know what big hotel he was staying in and where he traveled. At times, I wore the same clothes because I didn't change clothes from day to day. I hung up the phone and cried. My brother became ill. The Lord brought him back down before his death. He moved from California back to Louisiana. He was always a big drinker. He carried large bottles of liquor in the trunk of his car. I prayed and asked God to taste alcohol out of his mouth. God answered my prayer. I thank God he lived until he was ninety. God gave him a chance to change.

I moved into my first house for my family. My husband continued to abuse me. He still gave me $10 for food and no more. He cashed his check at the bank and always requested $5 and $1 bills. He did this to count out the exact change that was needed for a bill that was due. Then he pocketed the remaining of the money to spend when he went out with the boys and girls. He came home with lipstick everywhere and swore it was mine and I had not been near him.

I had to work to support my children. I continued to do housework for the upper class. After I cleaned, the finger test was performed. What do I mean by the finger test? The homeowners ran their fingers across the furniture to see if it was clean. My job was to dust, polish furniture, vacuum, scrub floors, clean bathrooms, and wash windows inside and out. Most women hid their mops so I could get on my hands and knees to clean the floors with a rag. Oh yes, I forgot about cleaning the refrigerator and stove all in one day. The homeowners paid $5.50, which was better than my previous pay of $0.50. Lillian and her group gave me $10.00. I learned how to pray and stretch my money.

Sometimes I needed a little more money to go with what I had. I asked my husband for a few extra dollars. He made me show him receipts. He never showed me his receipts. It was troublesome backtracking, trying to count what I spent at the grocery store and the children's school needs. He still didn't believe me. I would get my usual pop upside my head, and out the door, he went for the evening. He returned home at 1:00 or 2:00 in the morning. Some of the ladies I worked for were nice. Lillian had two boys that were just a little older than my two boys and a daughter that was a little older than my youngest daughter. Lillian's sister had a daughter that was a little older than my oldest daughter. All the ladies I worked for wore the same size clothes as I. during that time. I was smaller. They gave me clothes for the family. My children went to school looking nice, and we all went to church looking good. Every time I moved from town to town, God put good people in my life. God's goodness gave me hope.

I was at work, working in a new person's home. I was scrubbing her kitchen floor on my hands and knees. She was drinking coffee with her neighbor. I made a fresh pot of coffee and served it to the two of them. I thought to myself. I did that a lot. I asked myself, why are you down here on your hands and knees? You can do better than this. I thought I am young; I can read and write. I know how to follow instructions. In that instance, I decided to do better. When my shift ended, I went home. The next day I got up, went to the employment office in Inglewood. I set up an interview for the discount store in Manhattan Beach.

In July 1967, I went to the interview. The young man that interviewed me read my work history. He didn't see anything except housekeeping. He asked me if I thought I could do the required work in the store. If you give me a chance, I will show you that I can perform the duties; he gave me the job. Before I stopped doing housework, it was Labor Day; we all went to the park. My baby was about eleven months old. She laid around all day long, the day after the picnic. She followed me around and softly cried while I cleaned the house.

When her dad came home in the evenings after work, I told him she was ill. I thought it was something she had eaten at the park. Maybe we should take her to the hospital to make sure it was nothing serious. The doctor checked her out, and all of a sudden, they were running around like wild folks. I even made an unwise statement. They are running around like grand central station. I didn't know they were trying to save my baby's life. The doctor told me they were going to keep her overnight. She had meningitis. I had never heard of that disease before. I didn't know what meningitis was. We left the hospital went home, and I didn't worry at all. I went to sleep, got up the next morning, and got the children off to school. Then I went to work. Sometimes I took my youngest daughter to Lillian's house with me. Ash asked, where is the baby? I made the coffee, and Lillian cooked the breakfast. I told her she was in the hospital. She was diagnosed with meningitis. Lillian looked at me with a strange facial expression and asked, what are you doing here? I replied I came to work. She said, you don't know how sick your baby is? Get up right now and see about your baby.

I went to the hospital and found out not many people survive meningitis. I was frightened. I started praying to the Lord. Please don't take my baby. I didn't realize when I took her to the hospital. I made a crazy statement. Please, Lord, forgive me. For six days, my baby laid in the hospital lifeless. She didn't speak or move. When I visited her, I peeped in her room through the top of the door. She laid there and looked at me. She had tubes running in and out of her body. They were drawing fluids out and infusing fluids and medication in her body.

On the sixth day, when I arrived at the hospital, the doctor said she was out of the danger zone. I could go into her room. The doctor was afraid of the effects of the disease on her body. The doctor stood her up out of bed, and she was able to stand alone. She came running to me. The doctor said, thank God she is alright. She was not affected by the disease in any way. The doctor said if I had waited until the next morning to bring her to the hospital, it would have been too late. To this day, I still thank God for watching over us. When I went home and read everything, I could find about the disease. I became so frightened over what could have happened.

Now back to my new employment. The young man that did the interview looked at me in my eyes. He said, "I am going to give you a chance to prove yourself. You can report to work the day after tomorrow." I looked him in his eyes and told him you wouldn't be sorry. I felt I could do anything anyone else could do. I was always taught to don't look down and no scratching and moving around.

I got up the next morning. I put on one of my best-looking dresses and visited each of the ladies that I had cleaned their house. Lillian and her sister wished me all of the luck in the world in my new job. The other ladies asked me. You think you can do that kind of work. I told each one of them I'll make it! By the grace of God, and I did.

My new position paid $1.67 an hour. I worked there for almost two years. I found out from one of my coworkers they were getting paid over $2.00 an hour. Since I learned the position so well and how to do everything, I wanted the same pay. I was the only African-American working in the store. I spoke with the boss about my hourly salary. I waited, and they never decided to raise my pay. This was one of those stores that were a one-stop-shop. You could buy everything at this store, including food. I learned how to work the men, women, children, and the domestic department. I learned how to order, receive, and stock merchandise. I was also the salesperson for each department. Once I learned the department well. Then they moved me to another department. It was fun when I learned how to do the job. I was a fast learner. This gave me my self-esteem back.

I was working at the store when my 25th wedding anniversary was approaching. I wanted to celebrate. I told one of my coworkers about my anniversary. She thought it was a good idea. She helped me coordinate the celebration. I invited some of my coworkers, family, friends, and church members. I told my pastor I wanted him to renew our vows. I enjoyed organizing the ceremony. It made me feel so good about life ahead of us.

I bought a new dress; it was white, like a wedding dress. My coworker made me a veil. Everything turned out perfect. Everyone came and celebrated with us. My husband cooperated with everything. I thought maybe this might work out after all.

This happiness didn't last long. When I came home from work, my husband peeped out the window, ready

to start another fight.

I worked in the evenings. My shift ended at 9:00 pm. My husband still wouldn't let me drive the car to work. I had to catch the bus to work. The bus service stopped running at 6:00 pm. I rode with my coworkers until I purchased my car. I found an old car in the paper. The lady wanted $65.00 for the vehicle. My son and I worked swing shift, so our work hours varied. After I purchased the car, my son and I helped each other out. Whoever kept the car that day picked the other one up when their shift ended. That worked for a while until the old car broke down. My husband wouldn't even offer to let me use the car, not even on the weekend. I searched for a higher paying job so I could buy another car. My friend told me her employer was hiring. I went to the main office on my day off and got the job in 1961. My starting pay was higher than the top salary at my previous employer. We had been friends since my two boys were in their early teens. All my children called her auntie. The working conditions were better. My marriage was going down the drain. I was unhappy; my children were afraid for my safety. I knew I was going to have to make some changes.

I tried everything I knew to do to make things better. The children were getting older. My youngest son left home and married. My oldest son had gone to the Vietnam War and returned home. He had also met someone and moved out for a while, but he came back home. He and I worked for the same company but in different stores. The neighborhood we lived in, the children had gotten to know all their friends well. I didn't want to move anymore, but the pressure of knowing when I got home from work, I was in for a fight, and I was not a good fighter.

Easter was nearing. I always tried to fix things nicely for the children. My friend Ann and her family came down to visit us. What a wonderful surprise. She lived in Oakland, California. We were about five hundred miles apart. We always kept in touch. When I last saw her, she had two boys. Now she had a little girl. She was trying to catch up with me. After the trip, she had another girl, the same as I had, two boys, two girls. They spent the whole weekend with us. We used to visit Oakland before my parents died. We stopped by Ann's house to spend some time with them.

I decided that boxing was not my cup of tea. I wanted my divorce because someone would get hurt. I was trying to find the right time to tell my husband that I had enough. He had gotten hurt on the job and quit. He got hit in the back by the food truck that rode around through the plant at lunchtime. He had a lawsuit against the food truck company and his employer. Then he decided to make me leave his house. This was the house that the money came from my dad's estate. The home that he refused to pay the mortgage. I paid for it myself. But he said this is his house.

This was the house he never wanted. I wanted a better place for my children. This was the house he stopped paying the mortgage. I had to call the finance company to ask if they would allow me to catch up on the mortgage. They gave me that chance. We were three months behind in our house payment. The finance company was willing to work with me. I made weekly payments when I got paid. I was able to bring the payments current. The Lord was with me. I was not alone.

Chapter 13

My mother-in-law came to California to visit her children. Her boys got together and sent for her. My father-in-law was ill with cancer, not expected to live. The doctor said they had done all they could do for him. His mother spent time at each son's house. Everyone bought her something, but she had changed so much from when I was living with her. She started trouble in everyone's house while she was there. She spent time with her first cousin. She met some man while she was visiting. She told everyone she was going back home to Louisiana, and as soon as dad died, she would be back to stay. She went back home, and after she got there, it wasn't long that she had a massive heart attack and died. Dad lived about another month before he died.

My oldest son bought a new Chevy Camaro. When we got the news that she was in the hospital, all the boys took one car and tried to get there before she died, but it was too late.

They called back and gave the news to us. I took a leave from work and took my son's new car and drove to Louisiana. I carried my baby girl, my sister-in-law, and her son. When we got ready to come back home after the funeral, they packed food for us to eat on the road. It was hot in August. We didn't have an air conditioner, and we didn't have a cooler. I ate some baked ham and almost died on the road. It made me so sick. They kept stopping on the road to let me upchuck. I was no use to anyone for anything. We finally got to a town, and they bought me some medicine. It was two cars of us going back to California. I began to feel better, and no one else got sick. We made it home safe. About one month later, dad died, and they were back on the road. This time I didn't go. I didn't want to take off again so soon. I needed my job.

All this bad news came to my husband back-to-back. I didn't want to put him under more pressure, so I tried to hold off on the divorce. But he wouldn't stop hitting me. When my work shift ended, I didn't want to go home. My youngest daughter was at home. She loved her dad so much. He let her get away with everything. She didn't even have to do her homework when she was home with him. She cried, and he would say, leave that baby alone.

It was 1970, and another fight. We were separated, living in the same house for six months. He tried to make me go back into our bedroom. I only went into the bedroom to clean it or change clothes when he wasn't at home. I had made up in my mind that I would never sleep with him again. I slept in the room with the girls. He came into the den and told me to get up and go to bed. I said, No, I am not going in there. I was up watching a movie at about 1:00 am. He turned around, went to the kitchen, and open the drawer where I kept my knives. I saw him from the den where I was sitting. I don't know what he took out the draw.

I ran to the front door. He caught me at the door. I was trying to open the lock, but he was right behind me. My baby daughter, who was eleven-years-old, woke up my oldest son.

He slept on the back porch. He came into the house to help me. I had finally gotten the front door open. I was only wearing a thin gown, robe, and was barefoot.

I went out the door and off the front porch to the lawn. My husband was holding me in the back of my robe with one hand, and with the other hand, it went up over my head. I don't know what he had in his hand until this day, but he was about to stab me in the head with whatever he had. He later told someone it was not a knife; it was a meat fork. My son caught his hand in mid-air before he could come down on my head. I let both of my arms go behind me and left him holding my robe in his hand.

I crawled on the wet grass to get my balance so I could get up on my feet. I looked back to see how close he was to me, and I saw him turn toward my son. I got up running for my life. I ran about a block and a half from my house. I stopped and started banging on someone's door I had never met before. There were a young lady and a young man downstairs in the living room. The young lady called for her mother upstairs and woke her up. She told her there was a woman downstairs that needed help. Her mother said, let her in. She came down the stairs and asked me what's the problem. I was so ashamed. I was only wearing a thin gown. I asked her to please call the police. My husband tried to kill me. They became frightened, but they called the police. The daughter peeped out the window and saw a man walking up and down the street. I was so scared I was shaking all over. I thought my husband had followed me. I peeped out the window and saw it was my son. They open the door, so I could get his attention and let him come inside. The police came, picked us up, and took us back to the house.

They questioned my husband, and he told them we had a misunderstanding. I was still shaking because I thought they were going to leave me there with him. They asked me if I had anywhere to go for the night. I said yes, I called a close friend. She and her husband came over to the house, picked my daughter and me up, and took us to their home. The police stayed until I got a few clothes and they left. Again, I listened to family, friends, and went back to him. I never did trust him again. The fighting continued, but I decided I had to get a plan in place. It was hard for me to leave my house. Twenty-eight years in an abusive marriage was much too long.

While I was waiting to get a plan in place, there was an earthquake. It came about 6:00 in the morning. The girls and I were in bed. The rumble and the shaking woke us up. They started crying, and I held them close to me. The house was twisting, and things were falling on the floor. It just lasted for a short while. We got out of bed, turned on the light to survey the damage. There were cracks in the walls; the driveway was cracked and buckled. The border around the top of the rooms had dropped about two or three inches from the ceiling. Everything was calm when I was getting ready for work. As I drove down the street, I saw street damage. It was a massive earthquake. It was a six-point something; this is considered an enormous quake and can cause damage. I parked my car and walked into the store to get my usual cup of coffee. I couldn't believe my eyes. Just about everything that was on the shelves was on the floor.

In those days, there were no plastic bottles and jars. It was all glass. There were nowhere to step without stepping in glass and liquid. Everything you can think of on a grocery store shelf was broken on the floor. This was the worse mess that I had ever seen in one place. Everyone was standing around in amazement, wondering where to start cleaning up this mess. They had to close the store for a couple of days. They called every employee that was on payroll to come in to help clean. We were busy for a few days. This was fine with me. It meant more money and more time at work. When I left to go to work, I felt fine. When my shift ended, and I had to go home. I got a sick feeling in my stomach. I didn't want to go home. But my children were there, and I had to go home.

I went to Houston to visit my uncle. I had a lot on my mind. He and my aunt had visited me before. I went from

Houston to Oakland to see my niece and her family. My husband and the children were supposed to meet me in Oakland to ride back together. I sat on that plane. I asked for a window seat, and I just looked out the window and prayed in my mind, asking God what I should do? The only answer I could come up with was to get out of the marriage because there was no peace. I was not happy. When we got back home, I told the children my decision. My oldest daughter was in Oakland with my niece for a while. I called and told her I was going to leave her dad. She immediately caught the bus and came home. I told the children what my plans were and that I needed their help. They all agreed to work with me. It was close to Thanksgiving; he thought everything was fine. I cooked a real nice dinner for my family, but I had a plan. I told the girls the night before, when I leave for work tomorrow, pack what they wanted to carry and put it in their closet. I went into my walk-in closet next to the den, and I packed some of the things I wanted. We were going to leave the next night; the girls were out of school, so they had time. My son came home after 6:00. He would have made it home by the time we made a move.

The next morning, I got up, got ready, and went to work. All-day long, I kept thinking, Lord, let this work. I was nervous. I told my girlfriend what my plans were, and I was coming to stay at her house for a few days. As I drove home, my hands were clammy. When I got home, I fixed and warmed a plate of leftovers and carried it to the den. The plan was to put everything in the car secretly and drive away. My husband went to bed early and closed the door. He would not stay around and talk to no one. He never sat in the den with us and watched television, unless it was something he wanted to watch. We knew the routine.

I went to the closet and got a few more things for myself. I asked the girls; did they have enough clothes to last for a while? I did not know how long it would take before I could come back for additional items. The girls could go back at any time.

He went into the kitchen to get water every so often, to watch and see what we were doing. I set my plate on the coffee table, and we started to load the car from the back door. When I heard the bedroom door, we knew he was coming for water. We stopped whatever we were doing, and I picked up the plate as If I was eating. I was in the closet, getting clothes, sheets, towels, and whatever else we needed. The children had already loaded their stuff. I handed the bags to my oldest daughter, from the closet, and she gave the bags to my other daughter in the kitchen, and she handed the bags to my son, and he packed the car. I was packing things in paper bags for a fast getaway. We had an assembly line going. I learned that routine when I worked at the fruit cannery.

I took the plate of food with me. I didn't intend to eat until I reached my destination. Every time I heard the door, I would pretend to eat until he went back to bed. When we packed all, we needed for a while, the girls and I hugged my son, and we got into the car and drove away in the car that he didn't want me to drive.

I found a place after staying with my friend for a few weeks. My husband could no longer drive. He was losing his eyesight. I thought he would have his brother or friend search for me, but he didn't. He tried to fool the company with the lawsuit until he became ill. When he got his disability started, he stopped paying bills. It was ironic. The car he didn't want me to drive became mine, and I didn't have to fight to get it. I was working at the store; I made a decent salary, but I had quite a load to carry. I had to pay for everything with my paycheck. I was paying my car note, my daughters' car note, because she was laid off. I was paying the house note and all the utility bills, but somehow the Lord stretched my money, and I didn't lose anything. He called it his house. He knew they couldn't garnish his check because he was on disability. They would garnish my paycheck, but they never did. I always called the mortgage company when I couldn't make a payment on time. They always said it was alright.

Two of my friends and I rented a trailer, went back to the house to get some of my furniture. My husband told me I was not going to get anything. Now I'm not allowed to get the things that people had given me, and the other things I had worked so hard to obtain. When I left my house, it broke my heart, but I put my trust in the Lord and stretched out in his word. I worked hard in the past and never seen him fail me. I only had my two girls to be concerned about, and they were with me. I worked for every car we ever bought and was told I could not drive them only when my husband wanted to let me drive. I didn't feel any pain driving away in the last car we bought. He always wanted me to go with him to buy another vehicle.

In nineteen seventy-one, we went to court for our divorce. He asked his attorney to make me pay him alimony, but the judge said no. He was getting more money through the mail; than I was getting in on my paycheck. My attorney asks if I wanted half of the money from the lawsuit, and I didn't want a dime. I felt like he didn't want me to have any of it, so let him keep it. The judge granted the divorce, and I was finally free to live my life in peace. I was awarded the furniture that I wanted; I paid for it. Let him purchase his furniture from the money he was getting from his lawsuit. He could afford to buy more furniture. I asked my favorite cousin to come with me to get my furniture. They were like brothers to me. They were the brothers that I wish I had. They never turned me down. Anytime I called, they came to my rescue. I moved my furniture to my new apartment.

I moved often until I finally found what I wanted and could afford. When I call my cousins and said I need your help, they said not again. They came to help. I was glad I took the car. I needed it for work. I also needed it to pull the trailer. It was a gold and yellow hardtop thunderbird. He loved it. He would get in that car, get himself a cigar, and he thought he was in the seventh heaven, while I was sad and crying. My granny always said all good things come to an end. He could no longer drive. He would have let the car sit to be mean and spiteful to me.

In divorce court, I requested one thousand dollars from the house purchase. The judge granted my request, and I signed off on it. I took that money and found me a bigger and better place to live. I took the remaining of the money to pay off some bills. The money from the divorce helped me get back on my feet. I believed God would bless me with something better, and he did. A few years later, after moving from one area of town to the other, I tried to find a better school for my daughter. My brother offered to buy me a house if I kept his daughter with me. She was living with me. He brought her to visit. I told him I would keep her until he gets his life together. He was going through some problems. He married again, and his wife didn't want his daughter to live with them. She had one daughter, but she didn't want his daughter in her house. I thought about it and said, "No, thanks. Your daughter will never forgive you if you give her away."

I called my dear sister-in-law and told her she knew my brother had a daughter when she met him. I was not going to be the one to separate him from his daughter. Her mom was ill and could not take care of her. That's why she was living with me. He married this woman and dragging his daughter from pillow to post. I told her as soon as school was out, I was going to send her home. I gave her a few other choice words that you would not use in Sunday school. I had to let her know I meant what I said. I called my brother at the office. I told him what I said to his wife. I told him the last day of school was on Friday. I was sending his daughter home on a plane Friday evening.

I told my niece her dad wanted her to come home. I did not tell her that he didn't have the guts to stand up to his new wife. He bought a new home in Oakland Hills. I would not have her struggling with me when he could afford to give her a better lifestyle. I couldn't afford to provide her with a room of her own. My children had to share a room. He was going to take care of someone else's child and leave his child with me. I never told my niece the real story. Her dad and his wife finally separated. She died from a drug overdose. She was also an alcoholic.

A few years later, I bought another house that I loved. My daughter bought a house in the same area. She encouraged me to talk to her real estate agent. When my real estate agent and I were looking for a house, we walked into the house, one look, and I liked what I saw. I called my cousins and told them I had found a house I was interested in buying. They said to me under no specific terms were they going to move me again. I knew they were joking. They moved me for the last time. I worked hard and saved for the down payment. By the grace of God, I didn't have to ask for any help. My youngest daughter and I moved into the new house. I was still working at the store. My daughter was a senior in high school. I was an active member of the church I attended. I was the program chairperson of our choir ministry. I started dating a member of the choir. His wife died a few years before we started dating. One of my cousins was the choir treasure. My friend was president. We rehearsed on Thursday nights. After rehearsal, we all went out to a local coffee shop.

When the waitress saw us coming through the door, she put on an extra pot of coffee. She knew we were going to sit and drink two or three pots of coffee. We drank coffee and talked for several hours before going home.

My friend and I stayed a little longer. After leaving the coffee shop, we went home to our separate houses. This was the only time we sat down to talk about how we could improve the choir's funds. Every month the choir had a responsibility to turn in a financial obligation to the church. We paid dues each week, but that was not enough to cover the financial obligation. I planned a program to help meet our financial responsibility. We designed the program to help increase the number of people and money for the choir. My friend had three children.

I became close to his children. We dated for six years. He owned his own home, and so did I. My daughter did not like sharing me with his children. His mother disapproved of our relationship. I was a few years older than him. He met someone else and started dating her before we ended our relationship. We broke off the relationship. Men are the only thing I am not willing to share. Especially when I know about it, I had some restless nights. It took me about a year to get over the hurt. He finally broke up with that person. We became distant friends because of the children. They still wanted to spend time with me. They didn't understand what happened. I still cared for them as well.

In 1975 I moved into my newly purchased home. Three months later, I was in an automobile accident. My daughter was in high school. I injured my back. I could no longer work at the store and do the same duties before the accident. I had order drapes, carpet, furniture, and the whole ball of wax when this happened to me. I went over to my co-worker's house to pick up a beautiful plant she made to put in my living room. I left my daughter at home. She lived about fifteen minutes from me. I am glad my daughter was not in the car because I was hit on the passenger side's front door. If she had been sitting in that seat, she would have been badly injured or killed. The car was totaled, and I was left with a back injury. The plant was sitting in the front seat of the vehicle. It shielded my face from being cut up with the shattered glass. I only had a few pin scratches on my face. God was with me all the way.

The car hit me in an intersection as I was making a left turn and knocked me up on the curb. I had no broken bones. EMS transported me to the hospital, X-rays were taken, and then I was sent home. There was no one with me to tell my side of the story of the accident. The driver of the other car came over to see if I was alright. It was a woman with him. Someone called the police. We didn't have cell phones at the time. When the police officer interviewed us, the woman said she was driving, but I didn't hear her because I was in the emergency vehicle. I found out from the paperwork, there were some eyewitnesses, but I couldn't get names.

My daughter was expecting me to come right back. She thought I had just overstayed my time. I called my friend from the hospital, so he could pick me up and take me home. The next day I could barely get out of bed. I didn't know where to turn. I had a new home, new responsibility, and was not able to work. It took me about a year and a half to receive money from the accident. The insurance process was slow.

I had to go on state disability for several months. When I received my last disability check, I filed for social security disability. My youngest daughter and oldest son paid my house note until my health was better. My daughter finished high school at seventeen. She went one semester to Junior College. The doctor wanted me to have surgery on my back. I asked the doctor, "If I have surgery, would I still have back pain?" The doctor stated he couldn't make that promise. I told him, doctor, you keep your knife, and I will keep my pain. I didn't have surgery.

I continued to work at my church. One of my friends from church encouraged me to go back to school. I told her I was too old. I had four grown children. I wouldn't know anything. The younger children graduated from high school would make fun of me. She told me I would be surprised. I decided to give it a try. The children didn't know as much as I did. My desired major was social services. When I applied for social services because of my injury, I was treated horribly. I went back to the council office and changed my major to business administration.

When I applied for Social Service, they wanted me to bring receipts from where I had spent the insurance money. I explained the situation, but she didn't believe me. She wanted the proof, which I could not understand. I went home to get my bills. I kept all my receipts in a drawer. I got my adding machine. I added every receipt to make sure everything added up to eight thousand dollars. I put them into a brown bag, and I carried them to the lady in the office the next day. She was a black lady, but she turned a shade red when I gave her the bills in a bag. She said to me. I thought you had a checkbook. I told her since my creditors were waiting for their money, there was no need for a checkbook. Everyone was local. I received the check, cashed it, and paid my bills. I had already told them I was waiting for the insurance money. I just went and paid for everyone. You asked me for the bills, and I followed your instructions. She said I would have to get someone to sit and count all these bills. I wanted to tell her that I had to do what I had to do, but I didn't want to get smart. I needed some help.

A different worker came to the house and gave me a tough time. When I received the money, every one of the creditors filled my orders; drapes, carpet, furniture, beddings, and everything put on hold before the accident. That took all the money, but my house looked good. The worker came into my house telling me what all I could sell to get money, starting with my piano.

She made me feel like I had done something wrong. That's when I decided. If this is how I will have to treat people when I get my degree, I didn't want to be any part of Social Services. When the car insurance paid me, I bought another new Vega and paid the car off, so I wouldn't have a car note. They wanted me to sell the vehicle. I told the lady I needed my car

to go to school and look for work. She told me to go and get three estimates on the vehicle and show it was not worth over five thousand dollars. I prayed to the Lord. First, I went to the Ford Company. Then to the Pontiac. Last, the Chevrolet Company. I told them what I needed, and the reason I needed it, by the grace of my God, they all gave me what I needed. The car dealers all felt sorry for me. I told each of them how I got hurt. I have always worked and provided for myself. I paid my bills on time. I had good credit. I told them I was looking for work. They said they couldn't give me work, but they could give me a fair appraisal. I carried it back to the lady at the welfare office on time. I only had my car for a year and a half. It was like new. I waited for an answer, and another lady came out to the house to see if I had something to sell. Her first word out of her mouth after hello was, you can sell the piano; you don't need it anyway.

They finally gave me General Relief, which was one hundred and nineteen dollars and ten dollars in food stamps a month. I could not survive on that amount of money. I also had to go to the General Relief office, sit and give out supplies every day for hours. I didn't give up; I continued to hold my head up high, and I did what I had to do. This is why I learned how to depend upon the Lord for help. Because man will kick you when you are down, I realized the ladies that came to my house had to be jealous of what they saw. But no one gave it to me. I worked for it. I couldn't help that I was involved in an accident. When I bought the house, I did not depend on welfare. I depended on my job. I was so glad my family taught me how to work and not sit around and rely on others. I wanted nice things just like everyone else.

I went to the financial aid office at school. I applied for a grant. I was approved. This helped with school tuition and kept my bills current until I was able to work again. When the lady walked through my house, she made me feel so small about what the Lord had given me. I had no plans to stay on general relief no longer than I had to. I enjoyed working and taking care of myself. I was independent. I met men, but I didn't depend on a man. So, I didn't owe a man anything. I didn't settle for just anything.

Chapter 14

I.B. & Mildred
My Handsome Husband

My daughter did not want to go to school anymore. I told her

she had two options, either go to school or work. She chose

work. When she completed high school at seventeen, I wanted

to reward her for doing so well. I bought her a used car. I found out she didn't like it too much, but she drove it. She was dating this young man; he didn't have a job; neither was he going to school. I found out about it, and I punished her.

The young man had the nerve to come to my house and tell me to give my daughter her car back because it belongs to her. I don't know why she didn't tell him I was not that kind of mother who would let some young man come to my house and tell me what to do. I had to restrain myself from kicking him out of my house. I wanted to say some choice words to him. I told him to get up right now and get out of my house before I did something that I might be sorry for afterward. I know he was missing her rides, but that was too bad. The young man never came back again, and that was best.

She dated a young man that worked at the same place as me. He seemed to be nice to her. He took her out when he got off work. He came by the house before going to work. He picked her up and let her keep his car if she wanted to go somewhere while he was at work. I don't know what happened between them, but they broke up.

She met the young man she married. She waited until I went to bed. She would sneak to get the phone and go back to her bedroom. I woke up and followed the phone cord. I found the telephone under the cover with her while talking to this young man at 2:00 am.

When she quit college and started working, she saved enough money for a down payment on a new car. My daughter purchased a Chevy Camaro. I didn't have to help her with the down payment. She has always been a bright girl about saving money when she wants something. She was not so good at selecting men. The young man she married didn't want to work. He worked sporadically—they were married over twenty years. My daughter was always the breadwinner in the marriage. She had to support her family.

The house I bought was much nicer than the home I had to give up. In the scripture, I have always read that the Lord never allows anything to be taken from you, that he doesn't give you something better. I moved to a two-bedroom, one bath, a large kitchen, a breakfast corner by the window, a dining room, a large living room, an apartment in the backyard, and a two-car garage. It also had a large backyard cover patio. There were fruit trees in the front and the backyard. Peach trees, banana trees, avocado trees, and large lemon trees, the lemons looked like they were crossed breed with grapefruits, but it tastes like lemon. I couldn't have asked for anything better. My driveway held three cars, not including the two-car garage. I purchased my dream house. The prior owners had two sons. When the older son became of age, he wanted his own space. The previous owners built him a bachelor's apartment in the backyard. When my daughter got married, she stayed there until she bought her first house. I taught my children to work and be independent. When I started to work for the IRS, I had to stop school. I earned enough credits to get my degree, but they were split. I needed to do a term paper. I never went back to school after I started to work. I started off making good grades. I didn't want to fail English. I left with an incomplete in English. My highest-grade point average, while attending school, was 3.8. I refuse to let my GPA go down. 1979 my daughter married. I knew I had to find work. I couldn't keep depending on my children. The doctor told me I would never be able to work again. I prayed hard for that statement not to be true. I went back to my old job at the store and tried to work for a few days, but the pain was unbearable. My back wouldn't allow me to do the same type of work. I was enrolled in school full-time with 12 to 17 credit hours per semester. I searched for a job when I finished my homework. I found a job opening for an X-Ray Technician. I applied for the job and interviewed. The interviewer told me the work was too hard because of my back injury. The job required lifting and turning patients over. She asked, are you a

Christian? I said, yes, I am.

She told me to go home, read Psalms 37, pray, and write a letter to God. Put the letter in the Bible next to the scripture. She said, tell God exactly what you want. I knew I wanted an office job. But I had no experience. I did exactly what she told me to do.

The young man that directed the church choir worked with the Cedar Program Downtown L.A. I told him I needed a job. The program helped people find employment with little to no experience. He told me to go into the office, fill out an application, and put his name down as a reference. I did as he instructed. The receptionist glanced at the application, looked at her coworker, and whispered she has too much experience to go through the program.

The other young lady looked at the application and said in a low voice, no, she doesn't. The receptionist repeated, yes, she does. Her coworker repeated in a more aggressive tone she does not. She finally looked at my reference at the bottom of the application. They accepted my application and told me they would give me a call.

I received the call to come into the office. The job placement service called a few places to set up an interview. The placement center set up an interview for me with the Internal Revenue Service (IRS). I went down to the Federal Building for the interview. I met the lady. She showed me around the office and offered me the position on the same day. I followed the instructions the lady had given me to write the letter to the Lord. In less than two weeks, I had the job I desired at the Internal Revenue Service. I had to take a civil service test, and I passed it with flying colors. I also had to take a typing test, and I couldn't even type, they wanted twenty words a minute, and by God's grace, I passed that too.

My first position with the IRS was court cases. In this position, people who owed back taxes were summons to court to pay their taxes. I prepared the court cases for the attorneys. The documents for the court were transferred across the street to the courthouse. I learned the job fast. I worked in that position temporarily. The position was posted as a permanent position. They hired someone from the outside with no experience to fill the job position. They didn't offer me the position or ask if I wanted to apply. They transferred me to the file room in the basement. Someone suggested that I go to the union for advice.

I set up a meeting with the union representative to inquire about my rights. Most of my coworkers advised me not to go to the union regarding my supervisor's decision. She is the one that posted the position. Despite my coworkers', advice I had already talked to the Union Representative. He was waiting for my decision, whether I wanted to pursue the case. I decided to go forward with the matter. He told me that the service would have to pay me the position's pay rate or award me. I asked, which would be more beneficial? He said the award would look better on my record. It would help me to advance to another position.

The Union Representative contacted my supervisor to inform her that I had filed a grievance. She was furious, and so was her manager. The Representative didn't only get me an award; he also got me a $250 bonus. I started to apply for other positions within the IRS right away. My Supervisors didn't like me anymore. She sent me to the file room. She told me this is the position I was hired to do. It took a few days for the award to be processed. The girls in the file room laugh at me behind my back. They gave me the work no one else wanted.

When an award was given, a presentation was required. Everyone came to the supervisor's desk to see the presentation. The Union Rep gave the award and a check to my supervisor. She laid the award and check on my desk and said, here is your award for you. I said thank you very much. I didn't care how she felt. I earned it. A few weeks had passed, I applied for another position and got it.

I continued to apply for better positions. Every position was an increase in salary. My beginning salary at the IRS was a grade one, but the job they started me on was grade five. After I received my award, I was promoted to grade two. Then I moved to the Collections Department.

I met a young lady, name Mae. She trained me in my new position, and we became friends. We are still friends to this day. She told me that as soon as I learned the job, they would change the job description. I found out that she was right. There were new changes all the time. I moved up to grade four to the Bankruptcy Department. I continued to advance in grades. In three years, I was promoted to grade six. I was glad I went back to school. It contributed to my success in advancing to several different positions. I loved mathematics, and this was what I was doing every day, working with figures. There were no computers when I first started the job. The computers were installed about seven or eight years after I started. Bankruptcy was interesting. The work kept your mind sharp. When someone filed bankruptcy and owed income tax, they had to pay their taxes. The government always wants their money.

My oldest son Alvin lived at home with his dad. He was his dad's caretaker. Alvin was in a relationship, and they took a trip to Las Vegas for the weekend. While in Vegas, she played twenty-one. She won a lot of money, and they decided to get married while in Vegas. They called me to see if I wanted to attend their wedding ceremony. I said yes, I would be glad to come. She paid for me, my daughter, and two of her sisters' flights to Las Vegas. We had a grand time celebrating their wedding.

My son Gaines was on his second marriage. He had one son from his first marriage. He became an abusive husband like his dad. His wife called me for help. They often fought. I tried to advise her not to continue to take that kind of abuse. She called and woke me up late one night and told me I had better talk to my son, or she was going to kill him. I told her to go ahead and kill him.

When I hung up the telephone, I hopped out of bed and said, what am I saying? Supposed she does kill my child; I called her back; I talked to the two of them. Nothing seemed to help. He was quick-tempered, and so was she. He had a lot of his dad's ways during the first two years of his marriage. They were both too young to marry and start a family. They had finally divorced, and he eventually married again. Over the years, he has learned, and now he toned down and stopped the abuse.

My oldest daughter Dolores met an abusive guy. She bought a lovely home. The man she met was an alcoholic; he abused her and her son. I didn't find out about the abuse until her son Morroco told me. I couldn't do anything to help. She had to make up her mind and move out. She gave her friend a birthday party, and he invited his girlfriend to come. There was a fight between him and my daughter when he started drinking. She took her son and left him with the house. She was and still is the kind of person that will walk off and leave everything and never look back. I told her we would get the things I gave her. We moved almost everything out of the house while he was at work. She had bought the house. Why leave him everything for someone else to enjoy. After we moved everything out, she put the house up for sale, and he had to move.

My youngest daughter Dietra bought her first house. She worked very hard, but her husband was a drug addict. I never knew he was on drugs when they were dating. Children will keep secrets from their parents. She thought she could change him after they got married, but that never happened. Wherever he is today, he is still the same. He is a very goodhearted person, but he can't seem to get himself together.

This young man had no desire to work; he also drank a lot. They kept all this hidden from me until they married. She was still working for the telephone company. He was stealing money and food as fast as she brought it into the house. When they came around me, everything seemed fine. That was the way I did my parents. I covered everything up.

February 1978, just before my daughter got married. My daughter introduced me to a man. My oldest daughter had met him through someone she was dating. The two fellows were signing in the same quarter together. She was always trying to fix me up with someone. She told him about me and me about him. He was coming out of a bad marriage. I was fine living on my own. I had no one telling me when I could come or go.

He was a Christian and a preacher none the less. I had never dated a preacher before. He had six children. All his children were grown except two. They were teenagers. He and the children lived together. His wife would come and go unless she needed something. He was fed up with his marriage. He desired to start dating. His wife had someone else on the side, but he was focused on raising his children. We both were afraid to get integrally involved. When I met him, he said he would retire in five years and move back to Texas. His name is I.B. I didn't want to get emotionally involved if he went back to Texas. All my children were grown and gone on with their lives. I only saw the boys on holiday, and they didn't call too often. The girls came to visit. We went on a few dates. I thought if this relationship works, it might be fun moving to Texas. It was time for me to start a new life. I was living alone. I rented the back house. I always had to come and go alone. This was getting to be a little tiresome, even though I said I would never get married again.

I had two uncles living in Houston, Texas, which was not too far from I.B.'s home. He came from Galveston, Texas. They lived about fifty miles apart. I saw a chance for a new life. We dated exclusively for five years. After Sunday morning church service, we traveled from church to church to listen to local choirs and quartet groups sing. Once a month on the fourth Sunday night, the choir hosted a musical. As the days and years passed, we were getting to know each other. I said to myself, maybe this is the man I have been waiting to meet. We got along so well. He was somewhat different from the other men that I dated. He was not controlling, nor was he demanding. It was not all about what he wanted. He considered my feelings. I had been divorced for about seven years when I met him. I knew I needed someone to share my life with. After my husband and I divorced, I never wanted to bring another man around my teenage daughters. I continued to work in the church. I was now president of the choir. We had about sixty-five choir members. I worked with the Sunday school and the Missionary ministry. Our church remodel project was almost complete. My church was vital to me. I raised the assessment we contributed to the church.

Alvin, Dietra, Mildred, Dolores, and Gaines

Mildred, I.B. Singing with her Husband's
Family Singing Group in 1986

Chapter 15

After my divorce, I wanted to travel before committing to a serious relationship. Just in case the next man I met did not want to travel. I wanted to travel while living by myself. However, I was not particularly eager to travel alone. It would be fun to travel with someone. I am a flexible person. I love to have good clean fun, even at my old Christian age. I might get married again someday, so I decided to do a few things now.

When I was a child living at home in the country, I sometimes heard airplanes flying overhead. I looked and wondered where is that plane going and who was on that plane? What would it be like to ride on the plane looking down on the rest of the world? I thought I would never experience a plane ride. I thought this would be another one of my dreams. I used to dream I traveled from Louisiana to California on a slow train. I read about places in books and magazines and make-believe I traveled extensively. It took six days for the train to arrive at its destination. The train stopped at every whistle stop.

I never had the resources or opportunities to travel.

When we moved from Louisiana, we didn't go back to visit for twelve years. We traveled by car, and it took three days. We pulled over on the side of the road to take turns sleeping, or we stopped at a service station to let the children run around for exercise. We weren't allowed to do this at all service stations because of the color of our skin. We weren't always allowed to use their restrooms. We could buy their gas, food, but that was all we could do. My aunt died in Shreveport, Louisiana. I called my brother, who lived in Oakland, California, and asked, are you going to attend the service? He replied I am going to fly. I managed to gather money for a round trip plane ticket to go to Shreveport. My brother told me the day he was leaving. I arranged to meet him at our layover in Dallas. I enjoyed my first flight. I decided the next time I fly would be for pleasure. I loved flying until the 911 tragedy occurred. Now I think twice and pray before I board a plane. I am eighty-nine now, and I can run for connecting flight as I could in the past.

The opportunity came for me to take my first vacation. One of the choir members from church asked if I wanted to go to Hawaii. I hesitated for a few moments. I thought about my daughters. Then I said yes, I would love to go. I was not going to leave them home alone. I knew I could leave them with their oldest brother and their dad until I returned. This young lady and her brother's girlfriend were going on vacation to Hawaii. Wages were not as high, and airfares were not either. I was working and bringing home about one hundred and fifty dollars a week. I had two girls to support, and I had good credit. So, I leaped by faith. I didn't have the money, so I applied for a loan. The eight days' vacation to visit three islands costs $750. I started to prepare for the trip. First, I asked my son if the girls could stay with him and his dad while I was away, he said yes. I didn't always schedule vacation time off. If I didn't have a vacation planned, I continued to work.

Our first stop was in Waikiki, then Honolulu. This was my first stay in a hotel. When we drove from Los Angeles to

Louisiana, we only stopped for gas and restroom stops. I never imagine sleeping in a hotel room. I didn't have to get up early if I didn't want too. I could request room service. All of this was blowing my mind. Look what I have been missing.

Hawaii Trip

I tried not to seem so green and wet behind the ears. Once we arrived in Hawaii, we showered and changed our clothes. We went outside to view the beautiful scenery. We walked and rode city buses everywhere. We didn't know where we were going, and we didn't care. We wanted to sightsee. We had a car rental package we didn't use. We listened to people before we left home. They told us we would not have a place to park. I supposed the people that gave us the bad advice had never been to Hawaii. They were only trying to impress us. The information was false. There were plenty of places to park.

I immensely enjoyed my experience. We stayed in a beachfront hotel for three days. We relaxed in the evening and spent time on the beach in our swimsuits. We could walk right outside the door on the sand. I love good sandy beaches, and the weather was perfect.

Our next stop was the Island of Maui. Our three days there were more fun. We took advantage of our rental package and rented a car. We drove the countryside, met new people, and saw interesting places and things. We were free to do as we pleased. We went far out to see the sugarcane fields. The sugarcane fields were enormously large, and the canes were so tall you could get lost and hardly find your way. We grew sugarcanes back home on our farms, but the fields were not as large. The weather was pleasant, so it wasn't so hard for the workers to harvest.

As we rode around, some of the countryside look a lot like Louisiana. There were old farmhouses, large fields, and beautiful countryside. The country was not where I wanted to live, but nice to pass through for the view. We slept late, ate breakfast. We planned our tours for the day while eating breakfast. We dressed appropriately for the weather before exploring the island. We went sightseeing, rode around town and in the country. We stopped to buy souvenirs and eat lunch at some nice, exciting place while chilling. When we got back to the hotel, we relaxed on the beach. One of the girls could swim, but the other two of us could not. I liked lounging on the beach because the sun was not too hot, the weather was beautiful. I only put my feet in the ocean to take pictures. I knew it wasn't too deep. I turned my back to the ocean to give the illusion I was walking out of the ocean. I came home telling everyone I went swimming in the Pacific Ocean. The last part of our trip was Kauai Island. It was beautiful.

Hawaii Vacation

We had to fly from one island to the other. We loved touring all day, eating lunch, shopping, and sightseeing. On the island, we enjoyed traveling during the daytime and going to shows at night.

This was part of the good life I had never seen, dreamed, or expected. At that moment, I learn life is not always burdensome. There was something better for me to work and expect. All my life, I worked hard and only went to church. That was good, but God created a beautiful world for me to see and experience.

Dolores left home to live with her dad and big brother. It was just Dietra and me. She was my only responsibility. My daughter-in-law's friend wanted to take her three children to British Honduras for the summer. She said yes. Then she asked me if my daughter could go? I thought this was the opportunity that I had been waiting for, so I said yes. I was thinking about beaches, hotels, and the good life. I saved four hundred dollars; this was what she needed for the trip. My daughter called me and asked if she could come home, two weeks after arriving in Honduras. I said no, you just got there. She was supposed to stay the whole summer. I told her I had worked too hard to get the money; enjoy yourself. I was wishing I was there. She couldn't tell me the real reason because she didn't want the people, she was staying with to hear what she had to say about their place. When it was time for the children to come home, I went to pick her up from the airport. I started crying when I saw her. She began to cry. She was covered with insect bites. She said she lived out in the rural area of Honduras, not in town. Where she stayed, there was no modern convenience at all. She told me this was an old house, no running water, no bathroom. She had to go to an outhouse to use the bathroom. I felt so sorry that I misunderstood. I had to carry her to the doctor. It was a long time before she was well of all those scars. The doctor had given her medicine to take internally and to rub externally. I said never again would I send my child off with anyone anymore. She had taken pictures of the place, but when the time came for them to leave the place, she was in such a hurry until she forgot her camera. I had to make up for that trip. I continued to work and save my money. I had paid off my bills. I didn't want to borrow money from the credit union for a trip, even though I had good credit.

Chapter 16

Hawaii Trip

I planned a summer vacation for my daughter and me. I bought a new Vega Chevrolet to travel on vacation. My daughter wanted to take her best friend and neighbor on the trip with us. I asked her mother if she could come? Her mother said it was alright. I got a map and mapped out my route to travel to Sacramento, California. When everything was in order, we left Los Angeles on our way to Sacramento. Before we arrived, my front left tire went flat while driving sixty-five to seventy miles an hour. I spun out of control in the middle of the highway. The car turned around three times. I thank God there were no cars close behind. When the car came to a stop, I was in the middle of the divider, backed up in flowers, headed in the direction I was traveling. A man was sitting in a camper, a little way back. He immediately drove up to where we were and got out of his car to see if we were alright. He told me he was praying that the car didn't turn over. He asked, is everyone okay? I said, a little shaken up, I think we are.

I was fighting the steering wheel. It didn't want to steer straight. I later found out I couldn't navigate correctly because of the flat tire on the car's front end. The girls were in the back, screaming. We all were wearing our seatbelts. No one was hurt. The vehicle was not damaged at all. The nice man changed my tire, and we went on our way. He recommended that I stop at the Chevrolet dealer in Sacramento and change my tire because the car and tires were new.

We stopped in Sacrament at the Chevrolet dealer. They didn't have the brand of tire that I needed. Uniroyal tire brand was further down the road near California/ Nevada borderline, where I needed to exchange the tire. We had lunch and rested for a while. We found Uniroyal with no problem. They exchange the tire, and we were on our way. The weather was excellent, the highway was good, and we didn't have any more problems. Our next stop was Lake Tahoe. We arrived before dark. I had never driven through a mountain and deep revenge before. The children might have become frightened, but I didn't look at the deep slopes. I kept my eyes on the road. After checking into the hotel, we looked the place over.

The hotel met our standards, so we got changed, had dinner, and relaxed for the evening. The next day we were prepared to go sightseeing. We visited the taping of Bonanza. We had a real good time. We also went to Virginia City and Carson. The girls thought this was so much fun. They took pictures, so they could show their friends when they return. We spent one week between three cities. Our second stop on our trip was Reno, Nevada. We toured the city in one day. The next day we traveled to Las Vegas, our last visit. My friend and coworker from Los Angeles were going to meet us there.

The girls had fun when we arrived in Vegas. They saved their money to go shopping. They shopped and enjoyed sightseeing. Until they were tired, they came back to the room and order room service. I enjoyed seeing them have fun. That was one of the best times I had spent with my child. This made up for the bad experience she had in Honduras. My friend and I went to the casinos. I was never much a gambler. If I played ten dollars and didn't win, I would stop. I played the nickel machine. I went from one casino to another, looking at the operation of the casino and people watching. When I returned, my friend was sitting in the same spot where I left her. If she won, she sat there until she lost every dime. If I won, I was ready to walk.

Our vacation was coming to an end. It was time for us to go back home. We all drove back together. The girls were able to share their summer vacation trips with their friends when they returned to school. I also shared my vacation experience with my coworkers. It was time for me to go back to work, pay off some bills, and start another project. Life was going exceptionally well for me. I had a pretty good job doing what I loved. The store was a positive place to work. I had friendly coworkers that worked well together. One of my church members came into the store and said, you don't have that smile at church. I was there to make the customers happy. The store motto was the customers were always right. Our jobs were to make the customers feel welcome because we needed to sell merchandise.

I changed jobs, and each time I changed jobs, I received an increase in salary. My position at the IRS was a desk job and a step up in pay. I went to work professionally dressed every day. Now I see office workers dress casually. It wasn't like that. You had to look presentable.

I had another opportunity to go on another trip. My church choir director was friends with the director at the Music Center in Los Angeles. There was a Philharmonic Orchestra lead from New York. He came to Los Angeles to perform in concert when he met our choir director. The orchestra leader and choir director formed a black choir to take to Israel to sing with his band in Tel Aviv, Israel. The director sent letters to several churches in the city. He needed members to form a choir to go to Israel. Our director brought the news to our church. I had a desire to go. I had no idea how I was going to get $2,000. The trip cost $1,700. This included airfare, hotel, and food. I wanted to bring $100 for shopping. We were told not to bring too much money. I also needed $200 to get my passport and a few summer clothes. Most of the time, I had faith in God to help me; other times, my faith wavered. They named the choir "The Interdominion Choir" of Los Angeles, California, United States of America. The rehearsals started with two hundred members.

We were required to rehearse twice a week. Each month the number of members in the choir decreased significantly. Money was the problem for most of the members. I prayed I couldn't see how I was going to make it either. I started to drop out also. I went to the credit union where I worked. I applied for a personal loan, and the credit union denied my application. The credit union had approved me in the past. I was very disappointed. I called my I.B and told him what happened. I said I would have to drop out of the choir too. He encouraged me not to drop out to have faith in God. He didn't have the money to give me. He told me we would pray and for me to go back to the credit union. I said, what's the use? They will turn me down again. My faith was weak. The next day I went back to the credit union. I asked for an application for a loan. I filled out the application and carried it back to the loan officer. She looked it over and approved it with no questions asked. I went home walking on cloud nine. I called my friend and told him the news. He said I told you to have faith in God. I was anxious to go back to rehearsal because I had the money before the due date. The choir was down to sixty-five members, including the director and musicians. Our director, preacher, pianist, and I were the only ones from our church to go on the trip. Packing instructions was to pack lightly. I thought we would be there for fourteen days, and I don't want to wear the same thing every day. I wished I had taken their advice. I didn't need all the clothes I packed. We left Los Angeles on a five-hour trip to New York. My first time being in the Big Apple. I only got to see the inside of the airport. It was dark when we arrived, and I didn't get to see anything. We had had a layover in New York to our connecting flight for the Middle East.

We road on the bus to go to the international terminal, where we boarded the plane to Amman, Jordan. The flight was eleven or twelve hours. We all got comfortable. I walked up and down the aisle, ate, took pictures; we had fun. I was too excited to sleep. I knew we were flying over the oceans, but I was not afraid. We arrived in Amman, Jordan, in the afternoon. I always read about Amman, Jordan, and saw it on the news.

We checked into the hotel, settled in, and refreshed ourselves before eating in the dining room. The food looked good, but we were not accustomed to their way of preparing food; it looked better than it tasted. At an early age, my parents taught me to eat whatever was served for me until I could do better. We ate our dinner and went to meet with the tour guide. The next morning, we got up early, dressed, had breakfast, and boarded the bus to Jerusalem, Israel. We were surprised. It was a checkpoint at the border. We had no idea how extensive the point check would be. They performed a body-search on the ladies. Our luggage was emptied on the counter and thoroughly searched. When they completed the search, they threw our belongings back into the suitcase. We didn't have a chance to straighten anything out. The men had to go into a little booth, similar to the department store dressing room. The men had to drop their pants with their money belts. This is a standard procedure to check for weapons.

After the border checkpoint, we were on our way to Jerusalem. We arrived in Jerusalem midafternoon. We checked in our hotel room. Before we left the bus, the tour guide asked to keep our luggage locked because of thievery. They suggested that we rest until dinner, due to the long day set before us on the next day. Our leaders met with the tour guide at the station to get instructions for the next day. We were instructed to be dressed and ready for breakfast by 7:00 am and prepared to board the bus at 7:45 am. We boarded the bus, and the tour began as we rode along the countryside. As I listened to the tour guide, I began to think about what I read in the bible. I had

listened to the teaching and preaching in the church attended.

When I listened to the scripture's reading, I had no idea that I

would have experienced some of the places I had read about

one day. I had to pinch myself to make sure I was not

daydreaming. I thought if my dad could see me now, but he was

not fortunate enough to live that long. He never thought I

would ever go anywhere or be anything. I shrugged off my sad

thought and decided I would enjoy God's blessings. I began to

take pictures out the window as we drove along the countryside. I

also recorded some of the guide telling me where we were and

what we were seeing.

Summer of 1981. It was dry and warm like the summer

we have in the States. We were out most of the day. The guide

always let us stop and eat when we were hungry. I rushed back

and called home to tell my children what a good time I was

having. I couldn't wait to tell them what I had experienced in

the Middle East. I was excited and had conversations with other choir members. I was thinking back over my life up to this point. No one knew the changes I had gone through to get where I am. The sightseeing ended early, so we went back to the hotel, had dinner, and rested up for the next day. There was no television to watch. We just had a radio with the Arabic language. Some of the ladies ventured out and went sightseeing on their own. I was not quite that brave.

I was baptized in the Jordan River in Israel

Chapter 17

Breakfast was at 7:00 am. We boarded the bus at 7:45 am. Our director had to wake the late sleepers. Every day we had a different tour guide at each station in Tel Aviv. The tour guide told us where we were going. I was very excited to go sightseeing. Some of the places are where Jesus walked. After the tour, we ate dinner. The food was not bad. We just weren't accustomed to their food culture.

We stayed a week in Jerusalem, while there we toured: Bethany, where Jesus raised Lazarus from the dead. Bethlehem, the place where Christ was born, is now the oldest church in the nation. We viewed the basement; this is supposed to be the place where baby Jesus laid. They have a symbol there. We saw the stable where they tied the stocks while staying in the Inn, waiting to pay their taxes. We toured Jericho, where God told Joshua to walk around the wall seven times, and the walls fell. The site is called Nazareth, Jesus' hometown. We saw the city of David. The location of the Whaling Wall. People wrote down their wishes and stuck them on the wall. Some people believe they are waiting for the Messiah to return through the Arch of the wall. It is also known to be the Arch of the Temple of David. I attached a wish to the wall because I had the privilege to visit the wall, although I don't believe what they believe.

Mildred Israel in 1981

We visited the Sea of Galilee, where Peter started to walk on water. We explored Caesarea's city. We saw stones and pottery over two thousand years old; there was a fourteenth-century wall, built by Herod and reconstructed by the Crusaders. We visit Haifa. The guide said it was the largest city in Israel. This city is known for its diamond, import, and export factories. We visited the place where Jesus performed his first miracle, where he turned water into wine, the

Cannon Red Doom. We saw Mount of Temptation, where the devil tried to tempt Jesus. We visited the place where they stoned Stephen to death, and Bethesda's pool is where the water was troubled, and people were healed.

We travel to the Garden of Gethsemane; a church is in the garden. They welcomed us to go inside, kneel, and pray. This was scary and surprisingly emotional. Visiting the same place Jesus prayed, right before false accusations were brought against him by religious leaders accusing him of being guilty of a crime he did not commit. We participated in church worship service and the Lord's Supper at the tomb where Jesus' body laid. We also visited the tomb.

The tour guide waited patiently for us. It was dark when the tour ended. After the tour, he took us to dinner. We rested before we continued our tour to the Upper Room. The room was full of tourists. One of our directors started singing Amazing Grace; the whole choir joined in. The people stood and watched. The presence of God saturated the room. We all began to shout and praise God. We had church in the Upper Room. I could write a book on my experience in Israel. I was amazed to see places that I had only heard and read about in the Bible and other publications. This experience became life-changing. In the marketplace, the meat was stacked on the counters. The meat was in display cases like in the state. Upon the outside of this long counter. No meat case, no refrigeration. Some of the meat was hanging from the ceiling.

The weather was nice and moderate. We toured the Dead Sea. You can get in the water and float and never sink because of the water's minerals. I can't swim, so I took their words about not sinking. It was still a large body of water to me. Everywhere we went, people were standing with their hands out, begging something. Before being informed about the beggars, one young lady asked me for some clothes. I went to my room and got a dress and gave it to her. The tour guide told us she would be back tomorrow for more. We went to the River of Jordan. One of my choir members teased me about getting into the river. We were to get baptized, he said if I got into the river, he hoped I get bitten by a snake, he was trying to frighten me. He knew I couldn't swim.

The morning we were getting ready to go to the River of Jordan to get baptized. I didn't have the appropriate clothes for the baptismal service. When we arrived, I saw the water. I thought about what the choir member said, but when the guide talked to us about the place where John Baptized Jesus, and we were going to get baptized near the area, Jesus was baptized. I forgot all about the choir member's teasing. I had a chance to be baptized in the same river as Jesus.

Our director was also a minister. He did the baptizing.

It was like the baptizing that my folks did in the old days. Choir members were getting baptized right and left. I asked one of my choir members, my roommate, to use her wrap, and she said yes. When I went down in the water, I felt so light. I started shouting and praising God when I came up out the water. The minister told me after it was all over, that I tried to drown him. He had to have help to get me out of the water. I had a wonderful experience that day. We had church on the riverbank.

We completed the tour, it was now time for us to go to Tel Aviv, Israel, where the two concerts were. We boarded the bus and said goodbye to that part of our trip. It was a long bus ride. These tour buses were not as up to date as our buses in the states. The countryside is like our rural countryside in the U.S. I saw corn, cotton, watermelon, and many other vegetables growing in fields.

We arrived in Tel Aviv in the late afternoon on Friday. We checked into our hotel and rested before dinner. We went to bed early and woke up early on Saturday morning to go shopping. No one told us we couldn't shop. We found out all the shops were closed until six o'clock Saturday evening because of the Sabbath Day. We didn't have a tour guide. We were on our own. Tel Aviv is a more modern city than Jerusalem. Our first concert was scheduled at 7:00 Saturday evening. We rehearsed before it was time for the concert. We boarded the bus to take us to the park. Our first concert was in a large park. It's called an open-air concert.

We were the first black choir from the United States to sing in that city. The bus driver said it was about twenty-five thousand people in that park that night. It was dark when the bus picked us up. We could barely see. We were backstage, taking pictures of what we could. The mayor and some other city leaders came to greet us. We were in position on stage. The lights came over our heads. We sang as skillfully as possible. We exited the stage, wheeled away from the crowd, and headed back to the hotel. It was like we were someone special. I had a chance to see how celebrities feel. Sunday morning, we got up, had breakfast, and went to the auditorium to rehearse with the band. After the rehearsal

was over, the bandleader said everything looked good. The bus took us back to the hotel. We had lunch, and then we walked the streets of Tel Aviv, shopped. The stores are open on Sunday.

I bought two pairs of black dress shoes. We came back to the hotel to rest for the concert. The concert began at 5:00 pm. We were required to be at the auditorium at 4:00 pm. We took a group picture. After 5:00 pm, the curtain went up. The auditorium was packed. People were standing around the walls, in the isles, and the balcony. We took another group picture with the orchestra and the bandleader. What a day, little old me in Israel, feeling like a celebrity. When we finished singing, we whisked away from the crowd, escorted to the bus, and taken back to the hotel. We completed our mission. We rested after dinner. We were ready for the long bus ride to Cairo, Egypt. We left right after breakfast. It took a whole day to reach our destination. Cairo, in some parts, looks like our cities; some good and some not so well. We stayed in a nice hotel. We did some sightseeing. Our directors had already arranged for some tour guides to take us around. We had a chance to see the Pyramid and rode camels. We did some shopping and took pictures with some of the merchants We went to the museum as well.

The trip was coming to an end. I never thought life could ever be that good for me. It was time for me to get out of the clouds and back to earth again. It was time for me to come home to my friend, whom I had missed so much. I wish I could have taken all my children with me, where we could have all seen these things together. We boarded the plane in Cairo and flew back to New York and then to Los Angeles.

I had a good time on my trip. It was worth every dollar I paid and more. I would do it again if I could. I came home with plenty to tell. I took up sixteen rolls of film of the places we visited. I put all of the rolls in the shop together, and they lost two rolls in the film processing. I made a cassette tape of some of the tour guide speaking as we traveled. I made three tapes to keep for memory. One of my foster children recorded over one of the three tapes from the trip.

Los Angeles Choir in Tel Aviv, Israel

Chapter 18

After I came home from my trip, I had some decisions to make. My youngest daughter moved into her new home. I decided to start a new life for myself. My special friend, I.B. home, was in Galveston, Texas. He was going to purchase land to build a house on the property. This would be a desired place for me to live.

I went to Houston, Texas, on vacation to visit my folks. I also met his folks while I was there. I fell in love with the people and the place. It was my roots, southern living. I came back home and told my supervisor I wanted to transfer to Houston. I.B. five-year retirement plan was nearing to move back to Texas. I didn't want to have a long-distance relationship with him.

Over the five-year relationship, we had grown together. It would have been hard for me to see him go. I adapt well to changes. I enjoyed moving to new places and doing new things. When I previously visited Texas, my mother, two brothers, lived there. One of my mother's brothers died a few months after I went back home to Los Angeles. Then the other brother died a year later. They were one of the reasons I moved to Texas. I still had four cousins that lived in Texas.

I.B. and I were not engaged, but we were very close. We did just about everything together. He was a very kind, considerate of my feelings, liberal, and most of all, he didn't worry about me going to church, nor how long I stayed. He bought one acre of land. He took me to see the property when I was there on vacation. I had dreamt of what kind of house we would build together.

I went to Houston on another vacation. While there, I had a transfer interview at the Internal Revenue Service. The interviewer told me they didn't have any openings. I went back home and told my supervisor what occurred. I did not worry too much about it, because I decided to move anyway. My supervisor told me he could get me a hardship transfer if we had not heard from Houston, by the time we were ready to leave Los Angeles. God worked it out. He said he could get the transfer if we were engaged. I told him we were, and I knew we would be soon.

We planned to leave Los Angeles in the last week of October. My boss called me into his office and asked how long it will take for me to leave Los Angeles. He said they want you to come to Houston in two weeks. I told him I would be ready. They had opened a new Bankruptcy Department. They needed someone with experience to help lead the department. It was all new to Houston. They were making up things as they went along. The government moved grade seven employees and higher to another state with all expenses paid. I was not eligible because I was a grade six. My supervisor started the transfer process. When I came home from work, I called all my children to let them know my plans to move to Houston. They were all surprised and in disbelief. I called and told I.B. the good news. I put the house up for sale the next day. I picked up boxes and started packing the kitchen items.

I went to church, told my pastor and members that I was moving to Houston, Texas. This was a surprise to them as well. They heard me talking about moving to Texas, but they didn't think I would go after the church remodeling project. We celebrated by having a grand march celebration from across the street. The police stopped all traffic for us for the grand march. I only had a chance to sing with the choir two more Sundays before I left. The choir gave me my choir robe as a remembrance. I would never forget the times we had singing and working together.

When I went back to work on Monday, my supervisor informed me the transfer was almost complete. He told me they were going to move my belongings cross country, all expense-paid. The IRS scheduled the movers to come to my house the following Saturday. The moving company repacked everything I packed.

I.B. came over early Saturday morning. We sat on the patio and talked. I fixed lunches and drinks for the movers.

They had the van completely packed by 6:00 pm. We cleaned the house after the movers left. We locked the doors and said goodbye to my lovely home. My plane ticket came in the mail while we were waiting for the movers to finish packing. I had good neighbors. The neighbors that lived closest to the driveway were two elderly ladies. One of them was in her eighties and dating. She went out to dinner, the shows, and church on the weekends and didn't bother anyone.

The other lady was not as old as the active lady. She stayed home most of the time. She sometimes attended church with her daughter and spent time watching my house. She saw everything and everyone that came to my house. I don't know when she slept. She saw all of my friends and all of my daughter's friends. If anyone came around, she made sure to let me know. I like that about her. My teenage daughter could have had anyone hanging around my house while I was at work.

My children gave me a going-away party Sunday after church at Dietra's house. My children had their own families. All my children, grandchildren, cousins, friends, coworkers, and their families came to the party. We had a real good church service. I left town on Monday. The choir was exceptional to me, and I loved them as well. I took pictures and said my goodbyes to the members. I made cassette tapes of the last service. I was also sad to leave my church and friends. I served as president of the choir. I was the program chairperson, worked with missionaries, and the usher board for six years. I worked all over the church; it was rewarding to work in many departments and with different people. I will always have good memories of the times we had together. When I went back to visit, I felt sad because so many of my friends had died. Every time I go back, I sing for my friends. I.B. came to the party as well. Dietra had a cake shaped like Texas ordered for me. They cooked a variety of

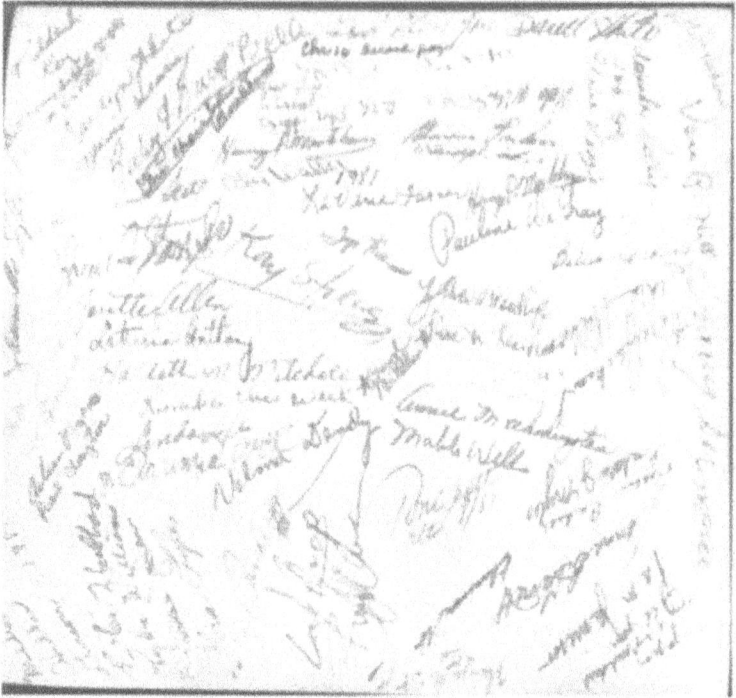

foods. The set table looked like a table in the movie "Big Mommas House." This was a party to remember. We took pictures and had lots of fun. When everyone started to leave, it got a little sad. Everyone was beginning to say goodbye. I thought to myself. My dream is coming true.   My children had not dreamt that I would move to Texas. They heard me talking about going, but they thought it would never happen. I stayed the night with my daughter after the party. My suitcase was packed. The only thing left to do was to go to the airport. My oldest son and my youngest daughter took off from work to take me to the airport. I felt sad leaving my children, but they all had their own lives. My daughter started to cry. I hugged them both and hurried into the airport. I got on the plane and found my seat, strapped myself in, and cried like a baby. It was time for me to live and make room for happiness outside of my children. I didn't want to leave them and go so far away. I would have preferred to stay close enough to drive to visit, but it didn't work out that way. I flew back to Los Angeles for almost every other weekend for several months.

Flight fares were cheap at that time.

My job paid for me to stay at the Adam's Mark Hotel in Houston until they found me housing. I stayed there for about a week. The hotel was just a short distance from my job. I could have a walk to work, but I rode the shuttle to work every morning and back to the hotel every evening. I arrived in Houston on July 11, 1983. I didn't know anything about traveling on government vouchers. This was my first experience. I had to learn a few things quickly. When I arrived at the airport, I called my cousin to pick me up and take me to the office. I had arranged to spend the night at her house.

When I got to the office, I found out they were waiting to pay my cab fare from the airport to the office. I also got paid for the day's work. My hotel reservations were registered at the Marx Hotel. The reimbursement for the cab was disbursed later. I stayed at the hotel. My breakfast was ready and waiting for me when I came downstairs. This was all at the government's expense. I had to call for the shuttle every evening just before time to clock out. The shuttle sat curbside, waiting to take me back to the hotel.

The office found housing for me, just across the street from where I worked. I looked out of my window and saw the office from the front door. I sometimes work ten to twelve hours a day to pass the time. I didn't know anyone that lived close by, and at the time, I didn't have a car.

Chapter 19

My 88th Birthday Party

I had been in Texas for about five or six weeks before hurricane Alicia came. I was living in an apartment alone. I didn't have a car; I had given my car to my youngest son before leaving Los Angeles. I didn't know the government would have shipped my vehicle as well as everything else. The Holy Scripture in Hosea 4:6 says, "My people perish for the lack of knowledge."

I heard the news media, and my coworkers say Alicia was in the Gulf. That didn't mean anything to me. I was from California, where we had earthquakes. I had never heard of a hurricane. They talked about it for almost a week. The day before the storm came to shore, they closed the office at 2:00 pm. I knew something was about to happen, but I didn't know what.

Someone told me to get a radio, some batteries, and some tape. I asked the question, what was I going to do with the tape? They all knew I was new to Texas. Someone told me to put the tape on my windows. I went to the neighborhood store and bought all three items. I asked the clerk what I should do with the tape? None of this made any sense to me. I went back to my apartment and looked across the street at other people's windows.

I put some tape across my sliding glass doors. I called my cousin to see what she was doing. She told me to come over to her house. I told her no; I would stay in until whatever they were talking about pass over. I had gotten my furniture out of storage, so I had a television. I watched television all evening. The news media said it would hit Galveston sometime that night. I called my daughter and told her I was fine, but I didn't tell her I was afraid.

I prepared something to eat. Then I finally went to sleep. I woke up about 1:00 am, and the windows were blowing, with heavy rain. My windows and sliding glass doors were shaking. I got out of bed and got my pillows and covers. I went into the next room, where the windows and glass doors were shaking.

In my living room, the sliding glass door was shaking so hard. I thought it would blow right out into the living room. I figured out why the tape was needed. I laid there, watched the television, and listened to what they said was happening, I wished then I had gone over to my cousin's house, but it was too late. The storm continued for several hours. They said it was almost to Houston. It was not lightning and thundering, so I wasn't afraid to watch television. I watched windows being blown out of buildings downtown. I thought my apartment building was going to blow away. I wished I had put the tape all over the windows to prevent the glass from shattering all over the room, but I had no broken windows at all.

About 7:00 am the winds finally stopped. Little did I know that it was not over. My daughter called me to see if I was alright. I said yes, I am fine. The storm has passed over.
I.B. called to see if I was okay. I said yes, it is all over. About an hour later, it started up all over again. I pulled the pillows off the couch and put them on the floor in my apartment hallway,

away from the windows. I could still see the television in the bedroom. The wind blew trees down, windows out of tall buildings, and furniture out of office building windows. I was frightened. I don't think I have ever been that scared before.

This storm continued until about 12:00 or 1:00 in the afternoon. When the storm stopped the first time, they said the storm's eye was right over ahead; that's why it was so calm. There was no lightning or thunder. It was just howling winds. I had never heard anything like that in all of my life. About 2:00 pm, the sun started shining, and the skies were clear like nothing had happened.

The weather was hot, and there was so much devastation. Our apartment building was not harmed at all. Many people were out of electric, some roofs were blown off, and trees on top of homes. Some people had to stand in line for days to get ice. I prayed I never have to go through a storm like that again. Whenever they predicted a storm in the Gulf, we left town until it was over. That was my get to know

Texas.

I.B. retired from his two jobs and came to Galveston, Texas, three and a half months later. This was just fifty miles from where I was living. All of his children were grown except for one son and his daughter. He had already moved her to Texas to live with his sister. I was delighted he was finally coming home. He sent for his youngest brother to go to California and drive back with him. He had two cars to bring back with him. A red and black dodge van and a little blue sports car. He hooked the vehicle behind the van, so they only had one car to drive. We didn't want him to drive home by himself.

They gave him a retirement party on one of his jobs. One of his coworkers drew a picture of the red van pulling the little blue car. It was in color. Every one of his coworkers signed the picture. It was so lovely of them. He kept the picture on the den wall for many years.

When he arrived in Galveston, I gave him a coming home party at my apartment. I invited all of his family. He was going to live with one of his brothers. His brother promised him that he had plenty of work for him to do.

After he was home for a while, we went to the bank to secure financing to build the house on the property. The property is located halfway between Houston and Galveston. It is kind of far from everyone. It was located in a tranquil and secluded environment. Some of my church friends call it in the country. I told him I would move out there if I could take all of my city's services with me. He told me I had too much concrete under my feet for too long; in other words, I had lived in the city too long.

When we went to the bank again, the Lord's hand was at work. We had no problem getting financing. The application went through, and I.B. had not even found a job. His brother wanted him to purchase an old house and fix up the property.

I told I.B if he built the house that I wanted, I would be willing to work hard and help him pay for it. I didn't want to live in just anything. I wanted something that we could enjoy together and bringing our friends to see. We went out and looked at an old house, but it would have cost as much to fix it up as it would cost to build a new home.

We went looking at new homes. My brother-in-law knew a fellow that built homes. He had hauled some materials for the man. We went to see the fellow, and he showed us some of the homes he built, and he was still building. We saw one house that we liked. We decided to build a new home. The builder did the paperwork, and we paid the earnest money down, which was one thousand dollars. The builder came out and looked at the property and began getting proper permits to build the house.

One day he thought about a friend name Earnest he had worked with in California. He moved back to Texas and bought a house on the Northside of Houston. Earnest told I.B. to come out to his job where he worked. This was another aircraft job; this was in his line of work. He went up to the job, and his friend brought him an application outside to fill out. My husband waited while his Earnest took the application back inside. He got the job.

My New Dream Home

They were working on the house all the time when we were having the other problems. On October 25th, they finished the house. My husband and I spent the first night in the house on the living room floor. The day we signed the papers, paid the closing cost, and received the keys. What a day this was. We were so happy. It was raining. The streets were muddy. The city had not opened the roads up. This was a problem for quite a long time. The house is a three-bedroom, family room, two baths, a dining room, a kitchen, a washroom, and a two-car garage. We drove out to the house every weekend, before it was finished, to visualize where we wanted to put the furniture. We took pictures from start to finish. We were going to plant a garden, fruit trees, and raise chicken. It was a lot of fun to see the progress made.

We moved into the house and enjoyed every moment. We planted trees, bought baby chicks, ducks, and a horse. My husband could ride a horse, but I never learned to ride. I never had an interest in learning. He tried to teach me, but that didn't work.

Our New Home 1985 League City, TX

He was riding one day, then he said, let me put you on the horse, and teach you how to ride. He put me in the saddle and started to lead the horse. I said, you are going too fast, he said I am just walking, how can I be going too fast? It looked like it was too high up off the ground. I was afraid I would fall off the horse, and the horse would run me over. She was a very gentle horse. I loved to pet her. My husband mated her with his brother's horse, and she had a pretty black coat. We kept the horse until we retired. The horse feed became too expensive. Most of the time, the horse feed bill was more than our grocery bill. Papa tried to teach our grandson how to ride. He was more afraid than I was. One day his little friend came over to ride the horse. He fell off the horse saddle. Every time someone comes from out of town to visit, they wanted to ride. It was fun to see other people ride. My husband kept the horse looking good. He tried to break-in the young horse to ride, but he sold the horses before he had a chance to finish the training. My husband began to have problems with his knees. It hurt him to ride the horse.

I'm riding a horse at our new home in
League city, TX

Chapter 20

My daughter Dolores was having problems with her son Morroco. He did not get along with his stepdad. My daughter talked to me about letting him come to live with me for a while. I spoke to my husband, and he said yes. We could make a difference in his life. When I was living in Los Angeles, he spent a lot of time with me. She worked, and I would pick him up when I got off. He stayed with me until his mother came home. I picked him up and carried him to church on Sundays with me.

He was a troubled child. His dad walked away when he discovered his mom was pregnant. He never got to know his dad. When he came to live with us, he got his dad's address from his dad's daughter. Morroco wrote and asked his dad if he could come and visit him, and he said yes. His dad lived in Dallas. I packed his clothes, and off he went. He was so excited to see his dad, and I was too. He didn't stay long. He called me and told me he was coming home.

When he came home, he was so hurt his dad had other children by his wife. Morroco was pretty heavy to be his age, and the children made fun of him. I don't know what else happened between him and his dad. He wouldn't talk about it. When he came home, his dad changed his telephone number. He was never able to speak to him anymore while he was with me.

Morroco my grandson

My daughter allowed her boyfriends to mistreat her son. When he started high school, he was in and out of trouble all the time. When he came to live with me, I took him to church every time I went. He got baptized and sung in the choir. My pastor gave him a lot of nice clothes. We went back to visit his mom, and he tried to take all the clothes to show his mom that he had a lot of clothes. She didn't buy him too much. My husband thought he was going home to stay.

He carried so many clothes.

His weight didn't change when he came to live with us.

He had plenty to eat at our house. He ate what we ate. Sometimes I found hidden food in his dresser drawer. I told him he didn't have to hide food. We had plenty. He told us the boyfriends ate all of the best food and had to eat canned soup and spaghetti O's. The children started to make fun of his weight at the new school. He began to get in and out of trouble. My husband and I were at work every day.

My daughter was a housewife. She didn't work at all. She should have taken more time to spend with her son. The stress was too much for my marriage, so I sent him back to his mom. I thought things would get better. I love him like a son, but I couldn't save him from bad company when I was at work. He learned to work computers when he was in ninth grade. His teacher said he could be a computer whiz if he wanted to. He was that good, but he didn't like that field of study.

I would have liked to spend more time with all of my grandchildren when I lived in Los Angeles. I worked fulltime, and they lived on one side of town, and I lived on the other side. My son Alvin has one daughter, Alvinya. She is studying to be a Journalist.

Alvinya Key my granddaughter

His wife was close to her mother, so she spent a lot of time with her. On holidays, they were the last to arrive for dinner, but I understood her reasons. After I moved to Texas, my daughter-in-law became ill. They found out she had a brain tumor, the doctor performed surgery, but she died. She never came out of the coma after surgery.

My son Gaines has a son, Gaines II, from his first wife. We have a good relationship. The marriage didn't last. The son is in the music rap field. My son married again and has two girls, Arlea. She is studying to be a nurse, and Ephrash, she is an attorney. His wife had two boys when they met. David is in the music field, and Ardeed is an attorney. I hear from the girls sometimes on holidays. They live out of state. Ephrash came to Houston once on business, and I saw her for the first time since she has been grown. After her mother and my son divorced, they moved out of state, but she did an excellent job with the girls.

Gaines married again, but that marriage did not last either. There were no children in this marriage. Then he married again to a young Indonesian lady. They have two boys, Yusuf Ishan and Sabir Zain.

Dietra had two boys, James, an electrician, and Jason. He is training to be a plumber. She bought them around often before I moved to Texas. After I moved, she had two more children, Danielle, and Justin. She brought them to Texas a few times to see us. I have thirteen grandchildren. All the children use to meet up at my house for the holidays when they were young. We fixed a big dinner; I always looked forward to cooking. We had fun. It would be nice if I could get them all together again, on a happy occasion.

I have about twenty-five great-grandchildren because all the grands are grown and have their own families. I think I have two great-great-grandchildren. I hope the best for all my grandchildren. There are many opportunities for them to have a good life if they pursue opportunities. Some of the children are not as ambitious as my children were. I hope they will realize what it takes to live in this age and time of life. Things have changed so much. I wish I had gone further with my education.

The children have all been such inspiration in my life. I do not know what I would have done without them. They were not bad children. My oldest son gave me no trouble at all. The youngest son was a little disobedient sometimes. The girls were alright. They could have been so much worse, so I am very proud of them. They always respected me and still do at their age. I love them very much.

**Mildred and Christeen at the church I
Attended from 1976 - 1983**

Chapter 21

After my husband and I retired, we started a maintenance business. We had to go to Galveston to set everything up. We had to get our business license and tax ID number. Someone introduced us to a person who helped us set up contracts with different companies. Most of the job sites were in Houston. My husband did not know very much about

Houston. We cleaned banks, warehouses, office buildings, etc. We hired his brother, sister, and another fellow to work with us. I was always a little afraid when we worked in banks. I thought someone would force us to let them come into the bank.

God protected us, and no one ever came around when we were leaving. Sometimes it was so dark when we were going to the car. During inclement weather, we got wet, trying to put the cleaning equipment in the car. Since I knew Houston pretty well, I always did the driving.

We thought we were going to make a financial profit from our business. The contact person that helped refer us to companies collected the money every month. I went to pick up the check for the month, and she gave me a check. I took it to the bank, and it was no good. I went back to her office, and she said she had not gotten paid for the month yet, and I should take the check back, and It will clear.

I took the check back the next day, and I still could not cash it. I drove back to her office. She had moved out of the office building and changed her number. We never found her. I kept the check for many years. I filed a claim with the state against her, but we never got paid. We experienced financial hardship for a while. That was the only source of income we had at the time. We depended on the income to pay our employees and ourselves.

We never got paid, and we had to let our employees go. We contacted each company and found out she had gotten paid for each of the jobs. We took some of the jobs ourselves. We found out we could work on our own. We worked for a while, but it was too much by us. Our grandson helped. It was not only

too much but also dangerous. We got behind in our bills for

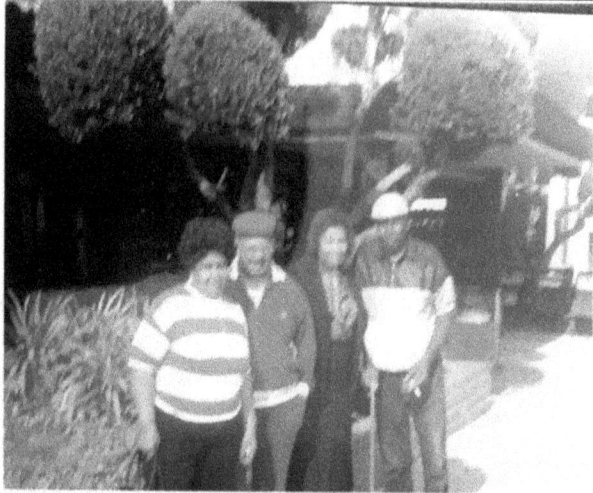

Visited Cousin Carnie & Frank in L.A.

the first time. I had to call my cousin in Los Angeles and

borrow $500. Then, my husband borrowed $500 from a friend

to keep from losing our home. By God's grace, we made it! We

finally let the business go. The clients we took on did not want

to see us leave, but it was for the best. We finally found work

and paid back the money we borrowed.

After Morocco moved back to Los Angeles, my husband and I were in the house alone. I felt a little lonely with the children being so far away. My husband started a family singing group. They were Quartet singers. I never cared too much for that kind of singing, even though that's what he was doing when I met him. I was home alone a lot. I wanted to do more with my life.

We returned from Shreveport, Louisiana. The church rented buses for transportation for the trip. We always went to Shreveport on Good Friday. Our pastor ran a revival, the choir sung, and some of the other members traveled out of town to support the pastor.

I overheard a choir member talking about fostering. She worked for Child Protective Services. She spoke about the need for foster parents. I thought that would be a good thing to do. Then I thought again, and I couldn't deal with my grandson. How would I be able to deal with someone else's children?

I came home and thought no more about it. Two weeks later, while preparing to go to Sunday morning service, the spokesperson was on the radio talking about foster parents were needed. Again, I said no, that's not for me. A few weeks later, the subject came up again. I said, Lord, are you telling me something? Three times I have heard the same topic within the past month. This must be confirmation. I finished preparing to go to church. I asked the choir member about foster parenting. She gave me the telephone number to Child Protective Service in Houston. I prayed, then I talked to my husband about it. He said if that's what I wanted to do; he will support me all the way.

I called the office in Houston and was given the number in my area. The person I spoke with told me the training class was getting ready to start for new parents. It was a ten-week class. We received all of the materials. We completed the course and received our certificate to foster children. My husband and I didn't agree with all of their methods, but I said

if that is what they wanted us to do, I could abide by it.

Mildred, Our Foster Child, and I.B.

I stopped to thank God for the way things were going for us;

for me, this was a new state, new husband, new house, and

now a new job. Who could not ask for anything more? I

didn't have to be alone anymore. The children visited

sometimes. My husband continued to sing.

I went to the doctor for my annual health check-up. My doctor ordered a stool test to take home. I never had one before. Two weeks later, I was scheduled for additional testing because blood was found in my stool. After I took the colon exam, I was diagnosed with colon cancer. My husband was having some health problems—what a blow at the same time. I had gone to Los Angeles on vacation. My husband didn't go with me. After I was there for a few days, he called and told me he couldn't pass all of his urine. I asked him did he go to the doctor. He said no. I caught the next flight home. When he came to pick me up from the airport, he pulled over, stop, and urinated in a urinal. I told him that he was going to the doctor the next day. We went to the doctor. The test results came back, and the doctor told him he had to have prostate surgery. He was afraid he might have prostate cancer because he had three brothers with the same problems at the same time, and they were diagnosed with cancer. His dad died from the same problem. He was convinced he had the same thing. We were both ill at the same time.

We started putting up a fence around our property. There was a whole acre of land we had to put the fence around. When we started working on the fence, we thought we had plenty of time to complete the job. We didn't know that we were going to be diagnosed with illnesses. We need the fence to protect our horse, chicken, and ducks from outside danger. Dogs and other animals were coming on the property. Plus, our horse was going on other people's property. We both worked every day. We both worked very hard with no help trying to complete the job. He was determined to put it up before he went into the hospital. We both had a doctor's appointment on the same day. I drove him to Houston. This was the day he received his surgery date. I had to get my test results. When the doctor came into the room, he sat down, looked at the papers, he looked up and said, you have colon cancer. He told me I needed surgery as soon as possible. It frightened me very much.

I got in my car and cried. I asked God, why me? He said to me so clear, why not you?

I got in my car, dried my eyes, and went to pick up my husband. I did not want him to know I was scared. I asked when the surgery is? He said its tomorrow. Then I told him my news was not so good. I told him we had to put our faith in God and believe that everything would be alright. My husband decided he had to complete the fence that day. I went out to help him work on the fence because neither one knew how long it would take to recover. I was in front of the house on my way down the slope. I stepped on a rock and fell in the ditch. When I looked at my foot, it was turned sideways up. It frightened my husband so badly; he was running in circles.

He could not pick me up out of the ditch because he was too weak himself. He said, I am going to the back to find something to make a sled out of, and I will hook the horse to it and pulled you out of the ditch.

I was lying on the ground, the Holy Spirit said, turnover on your knees and hold your foot up in the air and crawled up in the bank out of the ditch. I did just what he said, and I was out of the gutter. I called my husband and told him. I am out of the ditch. He came running, brought the car, helped me into the car, and drove me to the doctor. My foot was examined and x-rayed. I was told my ankle was broken. He said it was a clean break, no fractured bones. There was no break in the skin. He said I would have to have a cast on my leg and wear it for a month. He set my foot in place. I had to go back the next day to get the cast. We came back home and finished the fence that evening.

I couldn't take my husband to the hospital the next morning, so he called one of his brothers and told him what happened. Then he asked if he would take him. His brother dropped him off in front of the hospital. I was so upset; I couldn't go because I had to call someone to take me to get my cast. My husband had surgery, and the doctor told him there was no cancer. It was because of God's grace. They wanted to keep him in the hospital for a week. He said, doctor, I have to go home and take care of my wife. He stayed there for four days. One of his co-workers took off worked and picked him up and brought him home. We took care of each other. The surgeon postponed my surgery for a month because of the cast on my leg and foot.

My husband had to take it easy. He was on bed rest. I learned how to use crutches to get around. I wasn't supposed to put any weight on my foot at all. We waited on each other the best we could. One of my sisters-in-law came by to see us. She showed me how to pick my leg up when I walked with the cast. I tried to carry food in one hand, and the crutch in the other. I put my knee in a straight black chair and slid It across the kitchen floor. I became proficient at the chair sliding.

They took the cast off my foot after one month and put an air cast on my foot. I went to the hospital for my surgery. I had surgery. The doctor came into my room the next day and said, Mrs. Henderson. There was cancer on your biopsy. We went in to remove twelve inches of your colon, and nothing was there. Look at the Lord's work. I can't understand what happened. I said to him, maybe you don't know, but I do. The Lord healed my body.

One of my daughters called my former church in Los Angeles and told them about my upcoming surgery. I asked my pastor and the church members in Texas to pray because I was diagnosed with cancer. They prayed for me. That's when God healed my body. My pastor also came to the hospital and prayed for me before being prepped surgery.

After surgery, my daughter, Dolores, came and stayed a week with me. She left her husband at home to take care of the house. She arrived a few days after Thanksgiving. I was in the hospital on Thanksgiving Day. I could not eat anything.
After surgery, I had a lot of gas pain. My husband and some of my newfound church friends were with me.

The doctor wanted me to walk for exercise to get rid of some of the gas. It was hard for me to walk with the air cast on my foot. The nurses assisted me. My husband walked with me. Everyone talked about what they had cooked at home, and I didn't enjoy them talking about food because I was in too much pain. They couldn't give me any laxatives because of my colon surgery. That was the most challenging part of my illness.

I stayed in the hospital for a week. I had to pass gas before I could go home. I went home and stayed in bed for a short time. The therapist made me get up and walk. The doctor wanted me to get as much exercise as I could. It was better for my healing. I learned to get up by myself and do more for myself because my daughter had to go home. I learned to take care of myself, go into the kitchen, and prepare meals. That chairs sliding came in very handy. I could carry food from point A to point B.

Chapter 22

Our New House in League City, TX
October 29, 1985

When I first found out I had cancer, I decided to retire from the IRS at sixty-two. I made a withdrawal from my retirement. I had to take a cut in my social security benefits because of early retirement. After I got well, I got bored at home and went back to work. I couldn't return to the IRS; I had to repay the money into my retirement fund.

I found a job as a cook for almost a year at a nursing home. I saw so much wrong that I could not correct. The nurses woke the patients up and made them get out of bed at 6:00 in the morning. They were served breakfast at 7:00 am. When they finished their breakfast, they pushed the patients back in the hall. They sat in their wheelchairs until lunchtime. Then they moved the patients back in the hall until after dinner.

Some of the patients were so sick their heads were hanging out of their chairs. They did not put the patients back to bed because they did not want to lift and help them get back up for the next meal. They did not have enough workers to do the job well. When you are ill, you should be able to lie down.

The patient who could not get out of bed, the employees let their food get cold before serving them. I had to work evenings and weekends. I could not go to church when I wanted too. I could not be there to teach my Sunday school class.

I always went to Sunday morning service at 7:00 am. One Sunday morning, four buses came from Shreveport, Louisiana, to worship with us at church during the second service. I had to be at work at 11:00 am. Therefore, I missed the service. I got in my car, prayed, and cried because I did not want to leave. When I prayed, I asked the Lord to give me a job with better hours. The very next week, I went to Clear Creek School District and applied for another job. I got hired for food services at the local high school. The work hours were 6:00 am to 2:00 pm, five days a week—no more Sundays or evenings. Now I could go back to teaching my Sunday school class.

It was time for another physical. My doctor sent me for a mammogram. After the mammogram results came in, I got a call to come in for a biopsy. When my biopsy results came back,

I found out I had breast cancer. This didn't hit me as hard as the colon cancer news. I got on my knees, and I prayed to the Lord. They scheduled me for surgery. I was in the hospital for two days. I didn't have chemo or radiation treatment. What a blessing again, that's why I can say that God has been good to me.

When I was released from the hospital, I went to my cousin's home. She no longer drove, but she could take care of me at her home. My husband let me stay there one night. He was there early the next morning. When the afternoon came, it was almost time for him to leave. He told me he could take care of me at home. I got my little stuff in the bag and told my cousin I was going home. She said, you just got here. I wanted to stay a while longer, at least until my daughter came into town. I knew he was lonesome at home. I knew he could take care of me. He had taken care of me with my last surgery.

My youngest daughter came and stayed for two weeks. She and my husband got along very well; in fact, he gets along well with all my children. She helped my husband take care of me. She had a family of her own. She could not be away too long. A therapist was assigned to work with me a few days a week. They thought I was going to be depressed. When she came and talked to me, I was so upbeat until she said, you do not need any help. You are going to be fine. It would help if you had some physical assistance, not mental service. After the surgery, I could not raise my left arm. The therapist taught me how to stand facing the bedroom door and put my hands up as far as I could. The therapist helped with climbing the entrance; each day, I could climb a little farther, until I reach as far as my hands could extend. Now I can raise my arm again.

After this was over, my husband started to have problems with his back. He had a little pain, but now it was getting worse. The doctor gave him pain pills. I continued to rub him down at night. Sometimes I rubbed him down in the mornings, then he was off and running out the door to work.

This went on for a long time. Finally, the pain started to go down in his left leg. The problem got so bad until he couldn't stretch out in the bed.

The head of the bed had to be raised as high as it could go, and we had to do the same to the foot of the bed. The middle of the bed was lowered. We had an adjustable bed. He didn't want to have surgery. The pain got so bad one night until I had to call EMS. When they arrived to take him to the hospital, they put him on the stretcher. They had to work with him for a while before they could stretch him out. When we got to the hospital, the night doctor examined him and said he would be alright. You can take him back home. I became distraught and told the doctor that I would not take him home in the same condition when we came. They couldn't calm me down, so they had to keep him. He couldn't even sit in the car.

The doctor finally admitted him in the hospital. He stayed in the hospital for almost a week before he was better. After his examination by an orthopedic doctor, he was told he had to have back surgery due to a bad disc. They scheduled him for surgery and removed the bad Disc from his back. I didn't know that I could have gotten Home Health Care to help me take care of him after surgery when I took him home. I took care of him by myself. It was pretty hard, sometimes. After his back was healed, he went back to work. My husband had to retire early from his job; his hip began to hurt. He had been in a couple of automobile accidents, where he got some of those injuries.

His dad told him to stay out of the tree. He fell out of the tree. He got back in the tree again and went out on a limb. The limb broke. He fell out of the tree, standing upright. The doctor said that's how he knocked his hip out of the socket. He was afraid to tell anyone. He lived with his hip out of the socket until he was in his sixties. This was when he finally had to have surgery.

He retired from the aircraft plant. He had gotten a job at the same school where I was working. He suffered from the pain as long as he could. He went to the hospital, and they replaced his right hip. It was the worse one. He came through everything fine. He can now walk without a cane. We have had severe illnesses. The Lord has always been with us.

A Cake for my Husband in 1985

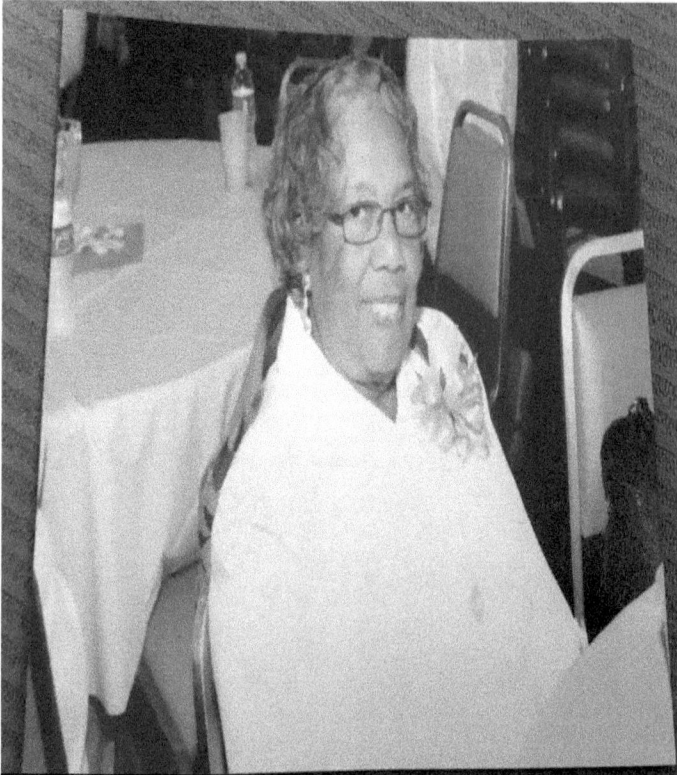

Sunday School Teacher for 29 Years

Chapter 23

I started to foster care after all the illness had passed. I began to foster children in 1993. I got my first child; she was eight years old. They brought her on Friday, and I sent her back on Monday. We picked her up from the mental hospital, that should have been a clue for me, but it didn't ring a bell. The social worker came, and she would not get out of the car for a long time. When she finally got out and went into the house, she stopped, looked at me, and asked how you would punish me when I do something you don't like? You cannot hit me!

I was a little caught off guard. I didn't know what to say. So, I said we'll see. She wouldn't do anything I asked her to do. We carried her to church that Saturday night. They were having a program for the children. They served pizza after the program. We picked up our granddaughter; they were about the same age. Everything went well at church. We carried our girl home, and my foster daughter asks me if she could walk with her to the door with my husband? I said, yes. Instead of returning to the car, she ran ahead and started running around the apartment complex. We must have run after her for over a half-hour before getting in the car. Sunday was alright, Monday she wouldn't get in the car to go to school. I had to have help to put her in the car. We drove to register her for school, and she wouldn't get out of the vehicle. I said, this is it, come pick her up. She broke me in for the job. I prayed to the Lord for help. When they called me the second time, I was ready. They brought me a brother and sister. The boy was twelve, and the girl was eleven. They stayed with us for about six years. They aged out when they became eighteen. I got several other children, while the two oldest were still with us. I fostered for eleven years. I carried the children everywhere we went. I got permission from the service and brought them to California on vacation with us. We had some good and bad times together. I enjoyed my job, it was sometimes trying, but it was all for the children's good. They needed to know that someone loved and cared for them.

The children were a lot of work, but so were my children. I treated them as if they were my own. There was after school programs, therapy, doctor's appointment; all of these things you would have to do for your own. They went to church every time I went. They worked on the usher board, sung in the choir, and they were all around children.

They did everything I asked them to do. Some of the children didn't want to go to church. They said I am not going to church; my big boy said, "Oh yes, you are. He was like a big brother to the younger ones. Once they started going to church, it was fine. Some of the children joined the church; they didn't want to go home when the service ended. I kept them from six months to one year.

We were always sad to see the children go when their time was up. Some of the children went back home to their parents after they had gotten themselves together. We had fifty-eight children to come through our home. I went to court. I met most of the parents. Some I just knew were not going to working out. The children were going to get hurt again. I wanted to adopt some of the children in my home. I accepted all races and ages, starting from four to sixteen.

We did so well with the teens until they most brought us, teens. Some of the parents would choose their boyfriend's over their children. We dress them well. I spent a lot of my own money on the children. The little money they gave me was not enough to take care of them. They made friends at church. I sometimes got permission to spend the weekend with their parents. My pastor and my church members love my children. Whenever they saw a new face, they said, Sister Henderson's got a new child, and they welcomed them. My children don't know a lot about my childhood life either. I have lived both sides of the fence. Segregation and after Integration. I know what it was like, what it was like to go to school and use books with no backs and missing pages. The books were handed down from the other race. We didn't ride school buses, county, or city buses. No matter how far we lived from school, bad weather or not, we had to walk. When Martin Luther King Jr.'s marches initiated, I was so afraid for our people. I was living in Los Angeles at the time when the march began. People were tired and ready to die rather than continue with the abuse they were taking. Everyone couldn't get out; some were afraid to leave. Some left and were afraid to come back home, even if there were a close death in the family, they tried to make you stay and not leave.

We went back to visit Louisiana in 1948. We were gone twelve years before we went back to see our relatives. My mother-in-law was a cook in a restaurant. We couldn't go inside to eat. We had to go to the back, and she gave us the food out the back window. We were paying for food. My boys were thirteen and fourteen years old. They didn't understand why things were like that. I had to explain the rules to them, and the why's. They grew up in California, where things were different.

When I moved to California, I thought I had died and went to heaven. Things were so different. I could ride the city bus and sit in the front seat. Right now, I won't go to the back of anything. I sit as close to the front as I can. If I ride the bus or a plane, I look for the front seat.

My children don't know anything about separation. When they experienced some of that now, it's new to them. When you are young and have children, you have to sacrifice to take care of your family. I am now eighty-nine years old. I started as a domestic worker when I left the cotton field. I didn't want to earn money the way I had, but it was an earnest day's work. I was taught not to beg nor sit and wait for someone to give me something.

When I worked in sales and for the government, I didn't mind going to work. Hospital work wasn't so bad, but nursing homes were more than I could stand. I prayed that I never had to go to one to spend my last days. Fostering and working in healthcare is fulfilling. I like helping someone. The dream of our people growing up was to become a schoolteacher if you wanted to get out of the field. I had a few relatives to become teachers and moved away to other states, and they lived well. They didn't pay well in the Southern states. That was a commendable job, and they cared for the students. They wanted them to learn. They only taught their color, not the whites.

My grandma told us. You can be whatever you wanted to be if you work hard enough and try. She didn't have a chance to do anything but farm, but I guess she also had her dreams. My dad always taught my brother to get on the largest farm and raise all the cotton you can. The cotton was going to the other folks. My brother didn't buy into the story. He caught a freight train and left the farm, family, and never looked back. When we all left the South, my brother started to do construction work. He got restless and started selling Real Estate. Dad told him to stay with the construction job, but he didn't take that advice either. He went on to become a top Real Estate Broker with his own office. My children never lived in the South, and they haven't done badly for themselves. I am very proud of all of them. One works in retail sales, one in outside sales, one in insurance, and the other in the top office of car sales they are not begging. With limited education, I think they are all doing well.

Collard Green Tree
League City, TX

Chapter 24

I started to write this book six years ago. So much has gone on in my life in the past six years. Let me tell you where I am now. I live in Los Angeles with my husband. He had severe pains in his left leg in 2011. He had two episcopacy surgeries on the same knee. It had gotten so bad; it was not only giving him a problem at home; it affected his work as a crossing guard.

I suggested that he see a doctor about his pain. He went to see the same surgeon that performed surgery on my knee. He took X-rays and told him he needed surgery because all the cartilage had worn out. He loved working. He did not want to be away from work; so, he scheduled the surgery for the end of the school year. The first week in July was the earliest appointment he could get when school was out. He wanted to be ready to go back to work at the beginning of the next school year.

He went to the hospital the day after the fourth of July.

The surgery went well. The doctor was very pleased. Later that same day, after the surgeon had gone home, he began to experience a lot of pain. The nurse gave him some pain pills. I stayed with him after the surgery. The problem got worse, and I didn't ask what they were giving him. I thought this was his surgeons' orders. They brought in morphine, and they showed that to him. This time I did asked what kind of shot are you giving him?

The next shift nurse came in to see him and asked how he felt? He told her he had some pain. She left the room and came back with something for the pain. I asked her what was she giving him? The next morning the surgeon came in about 6:00 am. I notice he was acting strangely, but I didn't know why. He took one look at him and went to the door, met a nurse, and asked, what did you all give this man? When he looked at his chart, I heard him say that this man is too old for this narcotic. He should not use these drugs. My husband had gotten sick to his stomach during the night. He had thrown up all over himself, and one of his monitors was disconnected. The doctor told the nurses not to give him anything else that he did not order. The doctor left and went on his rounds. The head nurse that worked the morning shift came to check on my husband. She asked how was he feeling? He said he was feeling just fine, but he wasn't acting himself. The nurse notices the monitor was disconnected, and she hooked it back up. She started to leave the room and looked back at the monitor. She ran out of the room to get a doctor. The doctor came in and examined my husband, and he went out of the room. They asked me to step out. I knew something was wrong.

I asked the nurse what was wrong with him. Then another doctor came into examining him. I asked this doctor what was wrong with my husband? He said to me my husband's heart is not beating; it is just quivering. I was afraid. I started to get concerned. I didn't want him to see me cry. He never lost consciousness. He was waving his hands at the nurses and doctors and saying everything is going to be alright. He didn't even know who I was. The doctor finally came and told me they were going to transfer him to the cardiac floor. Then I began to cry. One of the nurses hugged me and said he's going to be alright. I was still there from when he had surgery, and none of my children came to see about us.

I prayed to the Lord. Please don't take him. Give him another chance. I called his sisters and our children. I told them what had happened. When we got to the next floor, they went to work on him right away. They had to give him blood. He stayed out of his head for a few days. I slept right by his bed every night. Remember a while back in the book. When we have something, we have a big thing. I would take down all his vital signs when they came into reading them. When the nurse notices the monitor, everything was high. His blood sugar high, heart rate low, and his temperature were also high. He stayed in the hospital for two weeks. The musician from church drove us to the hospital. I left the car at her house, so I wouldn't have to pay the high parking price.

She brought me food. She picked me up, so I could go home to shower and change clothes. I had another friend at my church. She sent me food. My church members were my church family. My pastor prayed for us. My husband's pastor came to see him and prayed for him. His sisters got lost, but they came to see him. A lot of things he does not remember at all. This affected his memory in some ways. His daughter lives in Texas, and her family came to see him, but they had no idea how ill he was. I thought for a while, I would lose him, but God's grace kept him, and he made it through.

When the hospital discharged him, he still was fragile. I had no one to help me carry him in the house. I had one cousin that was willing to help, but he had a health problem, and he could barely walk. His wife was a nurse, and they stayed by my side. I would report all my husband's vital signs to her, and she would let me know his health condition. They were also there for me financially. I will never forget them. I love them like I love my children. I will always remember all the people that stood by my side.

I brought him home on a Sunday evening. The nurse told me to sit chairs at stations, where he could sit when he got tired. He had not had very much therapy because he had been too ill. He had gone for a short walk, the morning that I brought him home. When I got home, I got the walker out of the car for him to walk. I forgot to ask the therapist how to get him out of the car. The nurse put him in the car fine. When we got to the garage, I opened the door, and he put one foot out of the car. I forgot he couldn't put his weight on the other leg. When he slid out of the car, he couldn't get the leg that had been operated on to move. He started to go down. I caught his bottom in my hands. I began to pray and ask God to give me strength. He had one leg in the car, the other leg on the ground, and his behind in my hands. I knew if I dropped him, I was not going to be able to pick him up. My church family was not available, twenty-five miles away. We didn't know he was going to be released that day. God gave me the strength to hold him until he could finally drag the other leg out of the car. Then I had to hold him up until he could stand up. When I stood him up, he walked to the first chair and sat down. When I was ready for him to stand up again, he didn't have anything to hold. When we finally got enough strength to pull up, he was weak, but God had the power to walk him in the house and the bedroom.

I had to take care of him like a baby in every way. I learned how to do that in the hospital when the nurses disappeared at night. So, we made it through. He was not able to go back to work when school started. He didn't go back until after the next semester. When he was released to go back to work, management gave him a hard time. They made him reapply for his position, like a new person that had never worked for the company. They put him at a new school further for away. He loved the children at the previous location. He even received an award for his service; the children loved him. He went to work and worked the school term.

When he was working before, he had the knee replacement, he came home, change his clothes, went outside, and work in the yard. He went into the garage and did whatever he could find to do. After the surgery, he would just come home, get in his big chair, and sleep. The yards had gotten out of hand by the time school was over, and the weather was scorching hot. He came inside to get some water to drink and was pale. I was afraid he would have a stroke. I said to him, isn't this yard work getting to be too much for you. He said yes, but I don't have any help, so I have to do it. I asked him had he ever thought about selling the place. He looked at me and said no. I said it was just a thought. He said no, let's talk about it. We sat down and talked about it. I asked him if we sold the place where he would like to live? I knew he had a sister in Galveston, Texas. I thought he might want to live there near his extended family, but to my surprise, he said no, he didn't want to live there again. I told him. I know you don't want to live in Houston because he didn't want to live there when we first married. He said, you are right. So, I took a chance and asked if he wanted to move back to Los Angeles. He said that maybe a good idea. I said, don't say yes to please me. He said no, you're right; we are too far away from the children. When I saw he was willing to go back, I was so excited. I couldn't wait to call and tell the children. I called my daughter the same evening. As soon as I thought she was home from work, I told her we would move back home. She wanted to know what brought all of that on. I told her the whole story. She said to me, I wanted to ask you to move back, but I wanted it to be your own decision. One of the boys said the same thing. When someone got sick in California, we couldn't just get up and see about them, and when one of us became ill, they couldn't just come in the spare of the moment. After we told the children, we told our extended family in Texas. They weren't to please. Our daughter that lived in Galveston, was not too pleased. I knew what a problem it was for me to get help with my husband when he became ill, so I had to do what was best. We sat down and tried to work out where to start. We prayed, and then we began to get prices on U-Haul moving trucks. We had very little money, but I had a lot of faith. We needed enough money to continue to pay our bills where we were living, then money to move, and pay rent where we were going to live in California. That was quite a bit of money. I didn't give up. I started making calls to get things transferred, like bank accounts, medical insurance, car notes, put the house up for sale, etc. It was so much to do.

I called my niece in Las Vegas and told her we were getting ready to move back to California. She thought it was a good idea. She asked me how we were going to move? Where are we going to have our belongings shipped or U-Hauled? We couldn't afford the cost of having our goods shipped. She asked me had I gotten prices on driving. I told her, yes. She wanted to know have I finalized the deal, and I said no. She said, well, my youngest son worked for U-Haul, and he might get me a better deal. He might be able to get me his twenty percent discount as well. When she called me back, the price was almost one half of the price that was quoted.

After we finalized the U-Haul for transportation, it was on to the next step. We had two cars; one was going on a trailer behind the truck. I was going to drive the other vehicle. Everyone said no. Driving the truck from Texas to California is too much. One of my husbands' nephews said he would come with us and help drive the truck. Now my husband decided that I shouldn't drive the car.

I began to get boxes and start to pack. We had decided to get a one-bedroom apartment. Every day my daughter called and reminded me that we wouldn't have the large house we had in Texas and that I would have to downsize.
We had six rooms of goods, a storage house, and a garage full of goods to size down to a one-bedroom.

I told my husband that we should clean out the storage house first, then the garage, before thinking about what was inside the house. He began to price lawn mower, garden plow, extra bed, and tools in the storehouse. He had a trailer to carry the riding lawnmower. We worked so hard trying to clean out that place. Our daughter came up to help clean the home. She had a truck to haul our unwanted items.

When we decided to move, I said, let's leave in September. My husband said it would be too hot to drive across the country. My husband set a date for July 20th, which gave me about six weeks to get ready. I thought I would wait until we were prepared to tell my church family. I went to midweek service on Wednesday night. While I sat there, I felt I had been here for too many years to leave like that. So, I went up front and asked for their prayers. I said we had decided to move back to Los Angeles because of our age, bad health, and children.

The room got quiet, and I started to cry because I didn't want to leave my church family. My pastor said he understood. He called a committee together. He said they were going to give me a going-away celebration. They set it up for a Tuesday night. He said to bring food, but not to spend all of their money on food, because they would give me money as a going away gift. This celebration was one to remember for the rest of my life. The place was set up for a queen with my guest table. I received plenty of food, money, hugs, and well-wishes. The members at my husband's church gave him a surprise going away as well.

My one close friend, whom I had gotten to know like a sister, I was sad to leave her. My musician, Ione, is her name. She and her husband adopted me as their aunt. She helped me pack until everything was completely packed. They brought boxes, called, and helped set up the yard sale. I couldn't have asked for any more from my daughters; I will never forget them. I sold furniture, appliances, clothes, odds, and ends. Then everyone decided I would not drive my car, so at the last minute, Ione's sister helped me get rid of a lot of appliances, then she bought my extra vehicle.

Chapter 25

My father-in-law, me, & my brother-in-law

I never worked so hard in all my life. I tried to get things

sold. We started to give away clothes, hats, shoes, and furniture

at the last minute. It was not enough time to try to sell

everything. The day we were going to have the yard sale, it started to rain, so that didn't' go over to well. We had planned to leave Thursday night of the next week. My husband and I were in the garage on Saturday. Betty was in the kitchen. We were still packing. He started to feel weak. He thought his sugar had dropped. I ran into the house and got a mint. He put it in his mouth, and it shot right out, and he passed out. I called inside for Betty to call EMS. EMS came. They checked him out and told him it was not his sugar; his heart rate had dropped to forty. They took him to the hospital. I went to the hospital and stayed until I found out they were going to keep him. Betty locked up the house for me. I came back home before night to change my clothes. I went back to the hospital and stayed until Monday. The doctor released him. I told the doctor we were scheduled to leave the state on Thursday, would it be alright for him to travel. The doctor said he didn't see any reason why he couldn't travel. My husband and I both missed church the last Sunday we were in town. I called my pastor and asked him to pray for us. When I thought about it, I am glad I missed church, because it would have just been too sad. The Lord knew best. We went right back to packing on Tuesday, but we wouldn't let my husband do anything. We began to get more help from my church, on the night before we left, the house was full, people came to pick up stuff they had bought, and I just started giving furniture away. My daughter called me, reminding me to downsize.

I still brought too much with me and had to give away more things when we got to California. The children were looking for an apartment for us. Our friends were looking too. Then our friends asked us to stay with them until we found a place. We took them up on their offer. God gave us the money we needed to travel and find an apartment. We paid for the first and last month's rent. We didn't ask anyone for a dime. My cousin Keith and his wife Sherry gave us money to travel. I will always keep them in my prayers. They treated us like we were their parents. They don't know how much we love them.

The last day we were there, we picked up the truck. I looked at the cab and thought we were going to be too cramped, all three together. I called for the utilities to shutoff on the last day. They disconnected the electricity at 8:00 am. It was burning hot. I called to see if they would give me one more day. They were going to charge a reconnection fee; so, I said no, and we worked in the heat all day long. We stayed the night in the dark and slept until midnight, but Ione and one of our local ministers wouldn't let us.

She called the minister, and his wife came out, and he drove the truck to his house. We ate and laid down and got a nap before we hit the road. One of my choir members also came out, and she stayed all day and worked in the heat with me. Those two ladies cleaned out that house before they left to go home. Thank you, Sheila, and Sabrina. I hope to go back to visit one of these days. That is a part of my family, which I miss very much. I realized we have gotten too old to drive the distance, but who knows what might happen. We left at midnight.

When I got in the cab of the truck, I couldn't stretch my legs. I knew I would have to sit somewhere else when we stopped for gas. I said I am going to have to sit in the car. The Dodge Charger was on the trailer behind the truck. They let me out of the truck and helped me up in the car. I was very comfortable. That is how I rode to California. We passed a policeman, and he just looked at me.

We rode through the checkpoint, I thought they would make me get out, but they didn't say anything. I turned on the ignition and used the air conditioner until the battery went dead, but it wasn't too hot. Everything went well until we got to Phoenix, Arizona, I heard a noise, my windows were partly rolled down, so I thought it was coming from the car driving next to us, but then that car sped up and moved on. My husband had a cell phone charger in the truck. He took my phone to charge it and gave me his phone. I tried to call him, but he had cut my phone off. I could not remember my nephews' number. I blew the car horn, but they couldn't hear it. On the Expressway, in Phoenix, I heard a banging noise, and I became frightened. I knew I had to get their attention somehow. I didn't know what had happened. I thought it was the trailer coming a loose from the truck. I called back to Texas to my sister-in-law and told her what I was trying to do. I asked her to call our nephew and tell him and my husband what I heard. They answered my sister-in-law's call and stopped to see what the problem was. When they stopped and looked, I asked did we have a flat tire? He said we don't have a flat tire on this side. That was the noise I heard; the tire blew off. We took the next exit and drove a short distance to a Taco Bell parking lot.

They called U-Haul; It was still daylight. They said they would send someone to bring a new tire. It took three hours for them to find us. By the time it was changed, it was dark. I was afraid to go to sleep. Our nephew took a nap, but my husband and I stayed awake. This was the only problem we had. He let my husband drive, and it was dark, but the Lord let him make it through. We arrived in California Saturday morning. I was good and tired and ready to get rid of that trailer. We were blessed to get thirty days storage free, so we drove on in and went straight to the U-Haul storage. We unloaded the trailer and took what we needed in the car. My girls met us at the storage place. Our friend that we had known for a long time made us feel welcome to stay at their house until we could find an apartment.

We arrived Saturday. Sunday our, feet were too swollen to wear shoes; so, we could not go to church. We went to our daughter's house and spent the day. Monday morning, my friend and her husband were going to take us apartment hunting. At the time, I didn't know my girls had taken off work to go with us. They were at the house before we were ready to leave. The group of us went looking. We went to several places, but I didn't see anything I liked. We went and had lunch, and the men were too tired to go out again, so we went and found a place. They asked me if I thought Papa would like it. I said anything I want he likes. I signed the lease. They had it ready to move in on the first of the month. This was what I wanted. We only stayed at our friend's house for ten days, and our place was ready. We rented the U-Haul truck again, and families helped us move. I am pleased. I think my husband is as well. His health is better. He doesn't have to get up and go to work anymore, even though he wants to. We still get up early and read our Bible and say our prayers. We are up sometimes about five o'clock in the morning. We can't get out of the habit of getting up early.

When I lived in Texas, I lived closer to my brother's daughter, who lives in Shreveport, Louisiana. I could see her anytime I wanted. It took about four and a half hours to drive to her house. I miss those visits. I could go back to my home state, Louisiana, and live well. With all of the changes that have taken place. Some die harder's in Louisiana don't want to recognize me as their equal, but it's like that all over the nation. It is a little cheaper to live there now than it is in other western states.

My younger son said to me after we visited Louisiana. I am going to one day go back and retrieve our land and build a house on it. I wish he could do that. No one else in the family had the resources or the time to get the information on the correct steps to take back the land. There were one cousin and my brother that talked to an attorney about the land. It would take a lot of money. No attorney in Louisiana would take the case, and the California attorney had no jurisdiction in Louisiana. Someone else is enjoying the benefits of my grandpa's labor.

My husband and I, after twenty-eight and a half years of marriage are still tugging together. We are still trusting in God and trying to help someone else whenever we can. Many people have asked how we fostered so long. I tell people we prayed a lot. Some people are afraid of young people today, and I know it pays to be cautious. There were times when I felt a little uncomfortable, but I knew the children needed a chance just like I did one day. Granny didn't give up on me. They needed love.

Everyone wants to be loved by someone. Suppose we could give the children a chance and an opportunity to do better in life? My husband and I were willing to take that chance. We sometimes hear from some of the children, once in a while. Sometimes one will call and sometime some will drop by to see us. Some of the children are good. Some went back to their homes and failed along with their parents. Some of the parents couldn't make it. Well, we are still in pretty good health as far as I know; we both even drive and keep up our church work. It's not always easy, there are times when things get hard, but we keep thrusting.

I made it through the storm and rain of life. I still sing in the choir. The pastor and some members of my former church call me hot rider because I drive pretty fast. We are just enjoying life. We hope to take vacations still, this time back to Texas. The children want us to stop driving across the country, and I think they are right. We will have to fly. There were times

in my life. I thought I would never be happy, but I am

delighted—what experience in life I have had. I was once told,

behind every dark cloud, there is sunshine. Asa Wesley

Sampson, my former pastorals, always sing, "There is a Bright

Side Somewhere." I am seeing some of that right now. You can

make it, young women, with God's help. Please don't give up.

Put your trust in God.

Mrs. Mildred Henderson

My granddaughter, Dietra, &

Mrs. Mildred Henderson

ACKNOWLEDGEMENTS

I am blessed to work with a very talented team. My editorial manager, April Johnson, has diligently worked on producing this book, wearing a variety of hats quite effectively. I am thankful for Alvinya Key and Morocco Curry, my editors. They know me so well and edited my writing with just the right touch. Finally, I am grateful to my publisher.

www.ingramcontent.com/pod-product-compliance
Lightning Source LLC
Chambersburg PA
CBHW060000100426
42740CB00010B/1342